165 Days of Combat

A Soldier-Turned-Medic's Diary of the 26th Infantry "Yankee"
Division, 104th Infantry Regiment in WWII

by

James A. Cutter

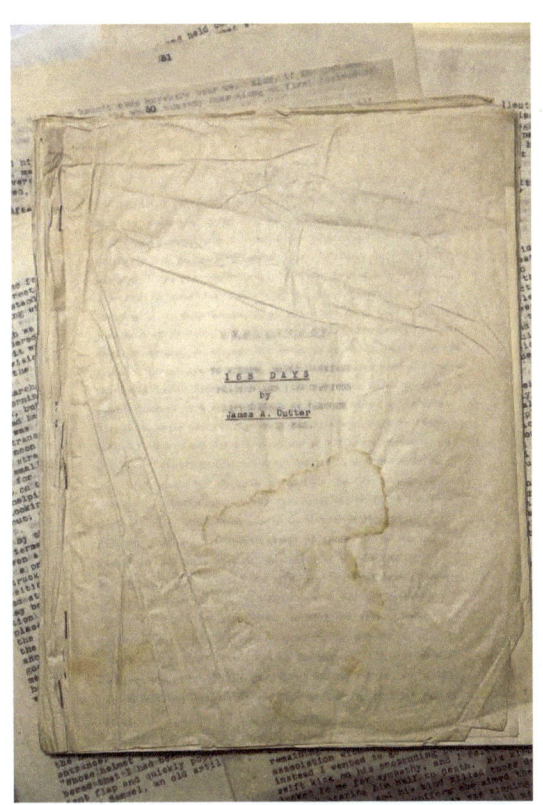

ISBN 9798999692917

For inquiries or to contact the author, contact:
jimcutterinww2@gmail.com

This book is a work of nonfiction. Names, places, and events are as recorded by the author and have not been fictionalized.

Independently published
Printed in the United States of America

Cover Photo Credit:
U.S. Army Signal Corps Photo SC 270909. Following an all-night attack in woods near Wiltz, Luxembourg, Infantrymen of the 104th Regiment, 26th Infantry Division, return to their positions, January 24, 1945. Signal Corps #ETO-HQ-45-8018 (Photographer: Gilbert), 166th Signal Photo Company, released by field press censor 1/17/1945. Original negative, Lot 10410.

Dedication

To my mother and father, whose constant prayers and inspirations safeguarded me
through this war.

Peuerbach, Austria
August 1945

CONTENTS

PREFACE

(by the author's son)

My father never spoke of the war.

As a child, I asked him questions about his time in service, but he never answered. Decades later, I asked again—this time as an adult. To my surprise, he quietly left the room and returned a few minutes later with a stack of yellowed pages. Those pages are the basis for this book.

After transcribing the original manuscript, I asked my father—by then in his seventies—if he would allow me to interview him further. I hoped he might expand on certain stories or reflect on a few memories. His reply was simple and final: "Everything I needed to say is in the book." He did, however, give me permission to publish the manuscript and later sent me the Prologue that appears here. But he never spoke of the contents again.

The value of this journal lies in its immediacy and authenticity. Many have documented the bitter cold of the Ardennes, scarce gear and rations, relentless artillery barrages, prisoner mistreatment, the chaos of friendly fire, the awe of seeing the first jet aircraft in combat, and the liberation of concentration camps. But few wrote these things as they happened—or shortly after—at age twenty, with no expectation of publication.

(The authenticity of these accounts is confirmed by an article my father wrote, published during the war on April 19, 1945, in the Webster News-Times, Missouri. The article, available in public archives, is reproduced on page 106.)

Though my father never spoke of the war aloud, I once saw him reading his manuscript quietly on Memorial Day. I asked him how often he thought about those experiences. He looked at me as if surprised I'd needed to ask.

"Every day of my life," he said.

Gary Cutter
Placerville, California

PROLOGUE

Moraga, California
August 1995

Apologia

It was August 1945, fifty years ago this month, when I completed 165 Days of Combat and mailed it from our small village in Austria to my parents back in the states.

The work actually began as a simple letter home, written in response to my parents' requests for more information about where I was, who my friends were, and what we were up to. Military censorship kept them in the dark about my actions and whereabouts for nearly eight months. From my army address, they knew that I was in an infantry regiment somewhere in Europe. The rest was up to their imaginations, not a very comforting resource in wartime!

Oh, I wrote my usual letters to them twice a week when combat conditions permitted. But I could write little more than, "I am well and hoping we can end this war soon." Even simple comments about the weather could attract the censor's razor blade because they might identify our location.

So, I promised to write some details of my front-line adventures in a longer letter at the war's end. 165 Days of Combat is the result. Upon completion, with 124 typewritten pages, I decided it was more of a book than a letter. So, I gave it a title, added a dedication, and mailed it home. My dad had several carbon copies made and distributed to relatives, but I had no desire to read them when I returned the next year. Besides, I had many post-war color slides with which to entertain anyone who wanted to know more about my experiences overseas.

It was not until early this year that I had enough curiosity and determination to unwrap the original copy of my letter, which my mother and sister had carefully preserved. And then: to read it from start to finish for the first time in fifty years.

I was surprised to discover how vividly the memories returned, together with all the original emotions of 1944 and 1945. I felt my heart racing as I revisited my first night in combat, with the pyrotechnics of tracer bullets ricocheting all around me. My teeth chattered again as I returned to sleeping in rain-filled foxholes in France and crawling through snow drifts in Luxembourg. Most terrifying was my return to the helpless feeling I experienced the day we were bombed and strafed by our own aircraft! I still flinch and reflexively look for cover at the sound of a single engine plane diving!

There were amusing, even happy recollections, too. I'm glad I included warm, human anecdotes to introduce several of my close buddies who eventually gave their lives to the war. Otherwise, the book would only be a necrology of forgotten men. That would be a great disservice to them, because that's not how they died. That's not why they were there. That's not why any of us were there, nearly halfway around the world from our loved ones.

My first reading left me with ambivalent feelings about the letter as it reveals the experiences, impressions, and prejudices of my youth. At nineteen, I was called up in the draft; was taught to kill the enemy and destroy his property during infantry training; was shipped overseas, given grenades and a rifle, and rapidly promoted in rank from buck private to first sergeant because others ahead of me became casualties of war!

I was amazed to discover how badly my writing skills had deteriorated during the intellectual void of combat. My grammar and sentence structure had been repressed to levels of rough immaturity, despite my years of experience correcting the copy of others as News Editor of my high school newspaper. But what else would you expect from a year of dehumanizing training followed by chronic sleep deprivation and living in foxholes like animals.

So, I put the work away to forget about it. This spring, during ceremonies to celebrate the fiftieth anniversary of Victory in Europe, I mentioned the paper to one of my sons, Gary, who asked if he might read it. Not only was he not repulsed by it, but he also requested my assistance in reproducing it for other family members. The copy you are about to read results from his efforts.

Caveat

Before you read my original letter, let me forewarn you about its contents. It is written in the vernacular of a guy barely out of his teens, who has just emerged from 165 days of 24-hours-a-day combat. Before going overseas, in addition to physical conditioning and expertise with weapons, he had been taught to both hate and fear the enemy. One basic fact was incessantly emphasized: in infantry combat, you will either kill or be killed! Whether by shrapnel, bullets, bayonets, or bare hands! No questions asked!

So, my letter reflects this base hatred and fear as an irrational prejudice against all Germans. Fortunately, I survived long enough for redemption from this attitude after the war, when I became acquainted with Austrian and German civilians as a member of the Army of Occupation. In considering my letter for Gary to copy, should I omit references to those prejudices and to other combat-related emotions? Should I clean-up the awkward prose and the endless compound sentences in order to conceal my intellectual regression during combat?

No, I decided against any omissions or alterations, preferring to leave it as originally written: a simple letter to fulfill my promise to let my parents know where I had been, who my friends had been, and what we had been up to. Typos, spelling errors, and glaring punctuation mishaps were corrected. But my awkward writing style in 1945 was edited only where it resulted in confusion.

Although the longest by far, this letter is just one of scores which I wrote to my parents during the war, including several dozen written during my six months of service before going overseas. Through those earlier letters, my parents had already become familiar with the jargon and military terminology scattered throughout 165 Days of Combat. But most of the terms are unfamiliar to readers fifty years later, so I have inserted bracketed explanations after the initial occurrence of each one. Otherwise, the entire letter is reproduced with its 1945 content intact: warts and all!

Finally, the letter seems to jump right into an ongoing narrative without providing a synopsis of what had happened to position me on the verge of going into combat. In the next section, I'll try to summarize several events which contributed to my status at the start of my letter

James Cutter, photo editor at Washington University prior to Army induction

This is a picture that we took for the Washington University yearbook, The Hatchet. Both the newspaper and the Annual were called the Hatchet because of George Washington and the cherry tree. I was Photo Editor of the Hatchet for the first half of 1943 before my induction. I had my own full-size press camera, a 4" x 5" Speed Graphic, which I am shown using here. The Hatchet yearbook also had one, but from the Zeiss Tessar lens, I can tell that the one I am holding is mine. After the war, I bought a miniature Speed Graphic, which is half the size of the one pictured.
Photo by James Cutter (shutter release by an assistant); caption by James Cutter.

Prelude to Combat

On Pearl Harbor Day, December 7, 1941, when our neutral nation was catapulted into World War II, I was only seventeen years old, a high school senior. My classmates and I felt confident that the war would end before we would be old enough for military service. After all, World War I had lasted only two years after the US entered it.

When military draft began early in 1941, only men age 21 and over were required to register. Surely it would miss us! We seventeen-year-olds felt confident our educations would not be interrupted.

By the time I reached eighteen, draft registration age had been lowered to include that age. But only nineteen-years and older men were actually being drafted by our local board.

By the time of my nineteenth birthday, September 22, 1943, some eighteen-year-olds were already being drafted. I was a happy-go-lucky second year pre-medical student: registered with my local draft board but classified 2-A because of my educational deferment. The War Department needed more doctors, so all pre-med and medical students were declared essential and required to attend classes 12 months a year. With that accelerated class schedule, I could graduate from medical school and become a doctor before I turned 22!

Unfortunately, the tides of war forced our country to change its plans for me. US troops had successfully invaded Italy, but German soldiers were being imported to reinforce the Italians. Hitler was already occupied with the Russians on his eastern front. We were on his southern front in Italy. What the allies needed was the creation of a third front for the Germans, thereby spreading them out even thinner.

For a new invasion, we needed more troops; lots more ground troops. Not doctors at the moment, thank you: our immediate need was for more infantrymen, preferably young ones, who are more apt to blindly follow commands in combat without hesitation!

And so it happened that my educational deferment was rescinded. In rapid sequence: I was reclassified 1-A by my local draft board, completed an all-day pre-induction physical exam, and was ordered to report for induction at Jefferson Barracks in South St. Louis, on March 31, 1944.

How clearly my first day in the army remains in my memory! Upon arrival at the Induction Station, I found the room to contain an absurdly heterogeneous mixture of cultures, economic levels, and social strata. Attire ranged from 3-piece suits to bib-overalls with straw hats! Dialects ranged from Ivy League to Southern Illinois twang. One older guy (at least in his mid-twenties) was an accountant, well dressed, with spanked baby-face complexion. Another was a coal miner with enough coal dust ground into his facial pores to prove it. Many had been farmers, recently displaced to cities in order to fill well-paying defense jobs, and still more recently forced out of their sheltered industrial deferments in order to meet draft quotas.

There were at least 200 of us in the receiving room, which had seats for about a dozen. After we milled around for an hour or more, a master sergeant entered the room, called us to attention, and told us to remove and place all civilian clothing in a paper bag, which was to be sent home. Never in my life, before or since, have I seen so many barefoot, lily-white, naked men standing in one room: all shivering and wondering what other indignities would come next. Were we all lily-white? Yes, racial segregation was the rule in all branches of the armed forces in the 1940's.

We were then ordered to line up in alphabetical order, a command which revealed that a significant number of men were not familiar with the alphabet. So the rest of us helped align them in proper order. Later in the day, we discovered that several were completely illiterate. That was all right with the army as long as they could sign official papers with an "X"!

The sergeant then marched us outside, still naked, to a long warehouse next door, where we threaded our way through the mountains of apparel which we would be wearing for the next two years. We were warned that from that moment until the day we left the service, we would be court martialed for wearing any clothing other than GI (Government Issue)! OD (Olive Drab) underwear was issued to us first, and we gladly put it on for warmth. Next came fatigue (work) jackets and pants, which we also donned. OD handkerchiefs, socks, boots and field jackets then made us warm again. Finally, we received our OD towels, overcoats, remaining uniforms, and toilet articles.

Everything fit easily in one duffel bag and became the sum total of all our worldly belongings. No privately-owned property was permitted on the post!

Laughingly called the barber shop, the next building contained at least a dozen straight chairs in a row, each one manned by a soldier with electric clippers clutched in one hand. There were no combs, scissors, or brushes in sight; just clippers, which were not even turned off between clients. The shearing of each inductee required less than two minutes.

We were now government property, just like the items in our duffel bags! They were GI, now we were!

Stepping out into the sunlight and lining up in rows to be formally sworn into the army, I made an amazing discovery: dressed alike and with close-cropped hair, we all looked the same! Despite differences in education, culture, and net worth, we were all beginning army life from ground zero. All God's children did look alike as new inductees, whether in the buff or in ill-fitting army uniforms!

After a week or so at Jefferson Barracks, several hundred of us were shipped out on a troop train to Camp Wolters, an Infantry Replacement Training Center near Mineral Wells, Texas, about 50 miles west of Ft. Worth. Like most hastily constructed military bases during World War II, it was built where a large expanse of unoccupied land was available. That usually meant in a location which was useless for anything else: worthless land, uninhabitable, remote from civilization. That's what it usually meant, and Camp Wolters was no exception. It was desert land, growing only cactus, sagebrush, and badly stunted scrub oak trees.

We were there for seventeen weeks of infantry basic training, which included comprehensive and intensive courses of physical conditioning, weapons training, discipline, military tactics, and motivation for killing Germans and Japanese. Anecdotes about Camp Wolters could fill a book, but this Prologue is not to describe basic training. So, I will restrict my narrative to several events which may help to understand our transition from courteous, social beings into mud-slogging infantrymen.

Camp Wolters was located in a hostile environment. We were fortunate having arrived there in April, when temperatures were moderate, and we could gradually acclimatize to extreme workouts in grueling heat. Before departing Texas in August, we would experience days with temperatures in the 120's! One battalion, with inductees fresh from northern Michigan, arrived in July and experienced three deaths from sun stroke in the first week of daytime training. As a result, all of us were forced to take salt tablets, and strenuous training was conducted after dark.

Our training company was divided alphabetically into squads and assigned to two-story frame barracks, each one holding 65 or 70 men. I was assigned an upper bunk on the second floor of that uninsulated barracks, a location which seldom cooled below 100-degrees overnight. That didn't interfere with falling asleep as soon as we hit the bed: our exhausting training schedule took care of that! On the upper bunk next to mine was a buddy who grew up only a few miles from where I did, George Binggeli. We helped each other survive basic training and continued our close friendship long after the war's end.

All barracks constructed during World War II are identical. If you've seen one, you've seen them all: a row of bunks lined along each long wall, with a clothes rack over the head and a footlocker (trunk) at the foot. Downstairs, at one end of the building, was the latrine containing five commodes, eight wash basins with shaving mirrors, a trough urinal, and five shower heads in an open stall. All fixtures were standard, and all had to be scrubbed and scoured each day before inspection.

We were assigned to latrine and other housekeeping and kitchen chores either in rotation or as extra duty for screwing-up. Floors were swept, and clothes racks and foot lockers arranged in a standard pattern for daily inspection. Beds were made up precisely each morning with square corners on the top blankets, which had to be drawn up so tightly that the inspecting officer could bounce a half-dollar off of them.

When addressed by anyone of higher rank, we responded with "Sir!" even if speaking to a non-com (non-commissioned officer: e.g. corporal or sergeant). We marched in formation everywhere. Some of our semi-literate recruits had to be given stones to carry in their left hands until they learned the difference between left and right.

Saturday morning was the most rigid inspection of the week, and the entire barracks had to pass it, or no one got weekend passes. So, we had a "GI Party" every Friday night. That meant moving all beds to one side of the room and scrubbing every inch of the floorboards on our hands and knees: then moving everything to the other side of the barracks and repeating the process. Posts and rafters were also scrubbed because the inspecting officer wore white gloves to check everywhere for dust and dirt!

We were restricted to the base for the first ten of our seventeen weeks, so none of us received passes to town at first. Instead, we trained seven days a week as we gradually built-up physical endurance. Starting the first week with simple five or ten-mile hikes, wearing light packs without weapons, we gradually worked up to full packs with bedrolls, tents, and weapons plus an obstacle course or two en-route to increasingly longer hikes.

The culmination of this conditioning was a 25-mile forced march with full weapons and packs. What weapon was I assigned to carry? Our sergeant ordered everyone six feet tall or over to take one step forward. I was six feet tall, yes, but throughout basic training my weight stayed at 133 pounds, so I was no heavy weight! We were then assigned to the weapons platoon, and I ended up carrying a heavy mortar on my back in addition to everything else! I was carrying two-thirds of my body weight on hikes up to 25 miles long!

Everyone smoked in the army. At first, I wondered why. One reason, perhaps: they were sold tax exempt for a nickel a pack compared with fifteen cents at stores. But that's not the main reason most of us started. It was because army psychologists had determined that peak training efficiency was maintained on a schedule of 50 minutes of training followed by a ten-minute break. So, the standard command after 50 minutes of training became, "Ten-minute break. Smoke if you've got 'em. The rest of you men, police up the area!" We non-smokers ended up working through every rest break!

It didn't take long for us to start carrying cigarettes in our pockets just to get a rest. Eventually we started lighting and inhaling them, and you can guess the rest: I was hooked for years to come. Not immediately, but subsequent combat and eighteen months overseas produced a strong attachment to cigarettes!

In addition to physical and psychological conditioning, we learned how to disassemble, clean, maintain, and fire every weapon used in the infantry. In fact, to qualify for shipment overseas, we had to practice repeatedly until we scored 80 out of 100 on targets. The weapons included: M-1 rifles, Springfield rifles, carbines, Browning Automatic Rifles, machine guns, mortars, hand grenades, rifle grenades, and bazooka rocket launchers.

We also qualified in hand-to-hand and bayonet combat, which we practiced on each other with scabbards covering the blades. On dummies, it was bare steel with ritual grunting sounds! No kidding: it was part of the drill, and we could do it in our sleep.

Several of our training exercises included hikes far into the desert for maneuvers, where we dug foxholes and simulated combat for several days, doing so in the heat of summer on restricted water allocation of two quarts a day for both hygiene and drinking. To test our fortitude as well as our acclimatization to foxholes, we were required to crouch down in one while a full-size tank rolled over us, then to stand up immediately and fire blanks at the vulnerable backside of the departing tank!

To complete our training and be freed from Camp Wolters, all of us had to creep through the infiltration course twice: once in daylight and once after dark, when tracers and shell explosions were more intimidating! This, too, was scheduled during our period of water restriction.

The infiltration course was set up in a field approximately 50-yards square with a row of machine guns along one side, their barrels locked vertically to fire exactly eighteen inches above the ground. They were unrestricted laterally, free to swing from side to side and sweep the entire field. Dynamite charges were buried in the soil every ten yards or so and were detonated remotely to simulate shell bursts as we approached.

Our job, using only elbows and toes: to creep across the entire field beneath the flying bullets, starting at the side opposite the machine guns, moving directly into the gun fire, and scrambling out through a trench beneath their muzzles. Using live ammunition, the machine guns were fired in bursts for as long as we were on the field. It was a real test of discipline and may have saved my life later in Luxembourg, as described in my letter.

Our company encountered a problem with heat on the summer day we were scheduled for the infiltration course. The temperature at waist level was 112-degrees. At one foot above the sand it was 122-degrees. And the sand itself was 140 degrees! So, shouldn't we postpone the course? Wrong! To prevent burns on our skin, we were issued heavy wool uniforms and leather gloves! So, we sweated a lot more but didn't get burned! Afterwards, we looked like sculptures in clay from the coating of sweat combined with dust raised by the explosions! A quick shower? Not out in the desert. On our limit of two quarts a day, we drank the water and retained our caked dust, running the course again that same night to add more to the coating!

James poses during bayonet drill – Camp Wolters IRTC, Mineral Wells, Texas

Camp Wolters IRTC, Mineral Wells, Texas. IRTC stands for Infantry Replacement Training Center, where thousands of us draftees were sent to be trained as fodder for WWII. On a map, it's between Dallas and Ft. Worth. The terrain and GI gear are genuine. The expressions were required for bayonet practice, as were barbaric grunts and shouts as we ran the blades through the midriff of a burlap practice dummy. Photo by James Cutter; caption by James Cutter.

Upon completion of our seventeen weeks of basic infantry training, we received orders to report to POE's (Ports of Embarkation) for shipment overseas as replacements for battle casualties. How well I remember sweating out those orders, hoping they would be for the ETO (European Theater of Operations) rather than CBI (China Burma India or Pacific Theatre)! They were for Europe, thank God!

But first, we were allowed three-weeks delay en-route for a last visit with our families before shipping overseas. My sister, Buff, and her newborn son, Bill, joined my parents and me in spending the time quietly at home and at our cabin in the Missouri Ozarks at the Coldwater Outing & Game Preserve. Her husband, Dick Thompson, had just departed for Europe as an X-ray technician with the 173rd General Hospital. Little did I realize that I would meet him in France five months later.

The time passed too rapidly, of course; and before we had time to adequately share our emotions, it was time to catch a train for Ft. Meade, Maryland. Most of my time there was spent in processing, receiving shots, and being issued all of the clothing and implements of war required by an infantryman.

My last two letters home before censorship reveal interesting insights into my youthful philosophy of life, which I summarized in my letter from Maryland, on September 25, 1945:

"And I believe my purpose in life is to help other people (as a doctor) in order to make the earth a better place for others to live in because I've been here. I say that I can do this best by being a doctor, but I may be wrong. God may have some other plans for me to accomplish my mission."

"Then why, you may ask, am I in the army now instead of in school? I think I know why: I'm learning more about people here than I could ever learn from any other place. And to me, being with other people is living! That's the only way I've been able to take and enjoy army life.

"My going overseas is part of my life, and I know it's going to be a wonderful experience. I'm going to learn more over there than I possibly could anywhere else. And it's going to help me become a better doctor when I come back. If it wasn't going to help me in life, why else would God send me over?"

My final letter, from New Jersey, dated September 29, 1944, included:

". . . this is the last really personal letter between us. I'll keep on writing more to you, but a censor will read them also. . . There are always two ways to look at everything, and I want you to always look at things from the most cheerful and reassuring side. I'm going to be looking at things that way, and I want to be able to feel that someone else is too."

Mother died in 1963, before I discovered that she had added a note to me in the margin of that last letter of mine. It says:

"You will never know how much these letters did help, Jim."

I do now, Mother.

165 Days of Combat now continues the story in my words of fifty years ago.

CHAPTER I

It was a rainy, miserable September day in 1944 when I left the peace and quiet of garrison military life and took my first step towards combat. Previously I had never been trusted with secret military information, and I had been free to tell anything I desired concerning my whereabouts and activities. Little did I know when I donned my new steel helmet and boarded that train for Camp Shanks, Orangeburg, New York, that I was closing a chapter of my life. As soon as the train pulled away from Ft. Meade, Maryland, an officer who accompanied us explained our new status. We had become a group of infantry replacements - each bearing a number instead of a name - traveling under an APO (Army Post Office) number instead of a post office address. We were all informed not to seal our letters anymore, for they would all be censored. That day we all experienced a series of different emotions: a mixture of anticipated excitement, regret, and homesickness.

Camp Shanks was designed to provide the first stage of adaptation towards life in the field. There we found the barracks to be of a cruder design with thinner mattresses, no pillows, and mess kits (folding metal eating/cooking utensils) used instead of china. With its elaborate Red Cross Club and proximity to New York City, Shanks could have been a very nice camp to spend several weeks in; but we were alerted and restricted to our own barracks area after the first day there. We were not even allowed to visit the six large theaters located on the grounds or attend church without an officer leading the group. Our last church service, a communion, was held early on the morning on October 4, the day we shipped to New York harbor and boarded that large, converted luxury liner, Nieu Amsterdam.

Of course, we, like everyone else who went overseas, were greeted at the pier by a GI (literally "Government Issue," GI can refer to both personnel and equipment) brass band and Red Cross ladies with coffee and doughnuts; but the cheerfulness they created within us was forgotten as soon as we saw the quarters we were to occupy for the trans-Atlantic trip. It consisted of a large room way down on "B" deck which had been fashioned by removing the partitions from several staterooms to form one large hall. Approximately 300 men were made to sleep there with a ventilation capacity for 15 or 20 people at the most. The ceiling was completely lined with hammocks, while the floor was covered with mattresses to provide sufficient space for the men to sleep. But that wasn't the worst part of it. The kitchen was located next to us, and all-day nauseating odors of ill-prepared food drifted into our crowded quarters, which already reeked with the stench of human perspiration and breath. It was small wonder that the majority of the men spent most of their time out on deck.

1

Because repairs were being made on the ship, we were unable to sail until the evening of the fifth. For security reasons they made us all go below deck so we couldn't stand at the rail to watch her pull out, but several of us managed to sneak up on deck and watch the skyline drift slowly away. It seemed like the farther away we got from the pier the larger the lumps in our throats became. We all had the same question in mind: how long it will be before I see these shores again. All of us knew that we were slated for combat, that many on the boat would not return whole, and that many would not return at all. It left a queer feeling inside of me as I looked around at the men nearby, wondering if it would be one of them who would not return, or perhaps even I.

It seems strange that the hopeless reality of death never occurs to doomed men. Perhaps it is much better, for if all combat men were detracted from their job at hand by the death premonition, there would never be a war won. Every man who goes into combat realizes that a large percentage of the men will never come out alive, but the thought that he will be one of those men never seriously enters his mind for more than a second or two. There is a standing joke among infantry men about such a situation. It tells the story of an officer informing his twelve-man patrol, which is just about to depart on a dangerous mission, that eleven of them probably won't come back. For some time, there was a long period of silence, when finally, each man turned to the rest of the group and sadly remarked, "I'm certainly going to miss the rest of you guys."

I was restless that first night on shipboard. The unbearable heat in my ceiling-slung hammock would not let me sleep. Every few minutes I would become disgusted, hop out of bed, pick my way along the restless forms on the floor, and sit in the cooling breeze by the open door on the promenade deck. I finally drifted off to sleep sometime after midnight.

The next morning, I walked out on deck to find a wonderful contrast with the day before. Instead of rain I found the sun was shining brightly, and all I could see for miles around was the beautiful green water overhung with cotton-ball clouds. I noticed that every five minutes we sharply changed our course and later learned that this was for protection against submarines. The external appearance of our peace time pleasure vessel had been changed by the addition of numerous anti-aircraft guns and a large cannon, the crews of which were kept on 24-hour alert. Yes, it was pleasant to tour the decks that first day and see beautiful green water everywhere, but later on in the trip I would have given anything just for the sight of land.

After we were out to sea two days the ship's PX (Post Exchange or convenience store) opened for our use. By standing in line for two or three hours we were able to purchase warm cokes, and then by changing over to another equally long line we were able to buy candy and cookies. Several of the more enterprising GI's who realized how much we hated waiting in lines bought the cokes by the case and set themselves up in business on deck, selling them for from fifteen to twenty-five cents each.

We were lucky to have on board with us a USO (United Service Organization, civilian entertainment) troupe which entertained on several occasions, but outside of that there was no recreation. Church services were held in the officers' lounge every two or three days.

After three days out, our course turned northward, and we noticed a continual increase in the roughness of the water. Several days we experienced storms which threw the ship at such an angle the promenade deck touched the water - quite a list for a vessel the size of the Nieu Amsterdam. Many of the men on board suffered from sea sickness

2

during the entire trip, but I was fortunate enough to be able to hold down everything I ate, which wasn't very much. In fact, the quality of the food served in the mess hall was so poor that for several days I lived on Hershey's Chocolate Bars. The last day on board they issued three "K" rations (compact meals for foot-soldiers' use in combat) to us for the trip across England, and several men were so hungry they bought them for up to eight dollars each.

We docked at the Port of Glasgow, Scotland, on October 13; and believe me, that was a sight for sore eyes! The harbor was so crowded we were forced to wait 24 hours for a ferry, but that period of time seemed like weeks to our anxious load of landlubbers! Upon reaching shore we were again greeted by the American Red Cross with what seemed like the best coffee and doughnuts I have ever had.

One of those quaint little Limey (British) trains with six-man compartments provided transportation to our camp in Northwestern England near Manchester and Chester. Camp Delamere Park, the replacement depot's name, had been a Limey marine training station before it was turned over to American use. Here again we became used to fewer comforts, for our bunks were constructed from crates with the bottoms improvised from the half-inch metal tapes used to hold the crates together. For mattresses we filled large burlap bags with straw.

It seemed the training program all of the replacement depots set out was designed to enrage us to the point where we would beg for combat duty. Every day we would be forced to take all of our equipment out into the pouring rain and lay it in neat piles on the sloppy ground, so some inspecting colonel could come around to view us in our misery. Another favorite trick was to make us put on all our belongings and stand at attention for an hour in the rain while some captain walked slowly down the line and examined each rifle. All of our belongings included: a rifle, gas mask, cartridge belt, bayonet, steel helmet, jungle pack, extra pair of shoes, extra set of ODs (literally "Olive Drabs," all wool uniforms) four extra pairs of underwear, three extra pairs of socks, fatigue pants, fatigue (work) jacket, field jacket, raincoat, canteen, mess kit, cup, eating utensils, two blankets, overcoat, rations, shovel, sweater, tow caps, shelter half (two shelter halves, when buttoned together, formed a pup tent), rope, tent pole, five tent pins, toilet articles, and a duffel bag (also folded and put in pack). Of course, this mess weighed well over 100 pounds.

Camp Delamere Park had several good recreational facilities. There were two movie theaters there plus two Red Cross Clubs, which served coffee and doughnuts every night if you cared to sweat out the never-ending lines.

About midnight on the 22nd we were ordered to board some more Limey trains, which took us to Southampton, our POE (Point of Embarkation) for crossing the channel. The coaches were not heated, and the weather was cold, so it was a pleasant surprise to stop at some dark, blacked-out station along the way and receive British coffee (Postum) and doughnuts from the English Red Cross.

Upon reaching Southampton we were surprised to see the bomb damage done to the city by the Germans in the earlier stages of the war. As we walked down to the pier, we saw many buildings that had been almost completely destroyed, and since that was our first real glimpse of war damage, it dawned upon us that war really was very destructive after all. Later on, we realized that Southampton had only been scratched on the surface compared to many French towns.

3

After more coffee and doughnuts by the American Red Cross at the pier, we boarded our ship for the voyage, the Antenor, a converted freighter. Our quarters were down in the hold, where the only conversion that had been made for human cargo was the addition of tables for eating. That huge room was to be our living quarters, dining room, and baggage compartment all at the same time. Twenty of us were crowded onto the benches around each table and made to sit there until after the journey began. I'm not sure just what time we did leave, for we were all so dead tired we fell asleep just sitting there. I don't believe the trip across the channel took more than eight hours, for we were just pulling into the beach when I went up on deck the next morning. It was still raining and rough, so we were forced to remain on the ship until October 26, when the sun came out and quieted the waves down enough for the LST's (Landing Ship Troops, for beach assaults) to come out and ferry us to shore.

The food served on the Antenor was just as bad as that on the Nieu Amsterdam - maybe even worse. One morning those Limeys had the nerve to serve us a pan of cold fish with the heads still on. We set the pan down in the center of the table, and the fish' eyes seemed to follow us as we moved around. It made us so mad we sent the whole pan back to the cooks, telling them to give them back to the king and also telling what the king could do with them!

The beach that we finally landed on was Omaha Beach, where our troops made their historic landing June 6, 1944. Evidence of the battle they had was still fresh around there, and the remains of scores of landing craft jutted out of the peaceful water at close intervals. The ocean floor was so covered with wreckage that only one or two channels were clear, and our LST pilot had to be very careful not to rip the bottom out. From the water's edge it was only about 200 yards to the steep, cliff-like hills, which were dotted on top with the remains of many pill boxes - Germany's West Wall. I was lucky enough to be appointed one of the guards for the officers' luggage, for the rest of the men had to climb that mountainous cliff and then hike about five miles with all their equipment on their backs.

In the group of men guarding the luggage was a fellow who had slipped on the boat crossing the channel and fractured his shoulder. Since they had no hospital on board, they just put his arm in a sling and told him to seek medical attention as soon as possible. Naturally the shoulder was giving him a great deal of pain, for he had no morphine or other narcotic to relieve it.

There were about eight of us altogether, and it was our job to watch the luggage until we could get a truck to transport it to the replacement packet's bivouac area. We were all very hungry until we noticed they were also unloading rations from the boats, so we "borrowed" a No. 10 can of peaches and two No. 10 cans of Chile con Carne. Then one of the fellows halted a truck and we all piled on.

We thought it would be a simple matter to locate the packet; but it was rapidly growing dark, and a record number of troops had been unloaded that day. Since no landings had been made for the preceding two or three days, they had rushed operations and made it a record day for debarkation. As a result, all of the bivouac areas had overflowed and no one, not even the permanent personnel, knew where any of the packets were located. New grounds had been opened for the troops, and no record had been kept of which packet had been placed where.

We traveled for miles over the countryside looking for a familiar face, but finally darkness forced us to give up in despair. The truck driver had to return to his outfit, so he let us off at the side of the road. After stumbling and falling into several foxholes we reached a spot of level ground next to a hedge row and decided to spend the night there. We heated up the last can of Chile con Carne and built a large bonfire to sleep around. The sky looked fairly clear for the first time in several months, so we didn't bother to pitch tents. Luckily though, I rolled up in my shelter half and tied myself in, for the minute we were asleep it started raining again.

When daylight came Cpl. (Corporal) Creech, the only non-com (non-commissioned officer) in the group, decided he would set out to find the packet while the rest of us tried to find something to eat. We finally perfected a technique for obtaining food: one of us would stop a truck loaded with rations and talk with the driver while the rest of the men worked over the back of the vehicle. I'll admit it wasn't exactly legal, but anything goes when you are hungry.

That afternoon we located the rest of the packet and joined them. Our bivouac area consisted of a large field which had been chewed into thick, oozing mud from the thousands of feet tramping the several months of rain into it. Nevertheless, we pitched our tents and made the best of it. From that day until the last of November I don't believe we had another clear day.

The food during our stay in Cherbourg hit an all-time low for us. General Patton had just finished his spectacular dash across France, so there was still an acute supply problem. All the palatable rations (K's and C's) were going to the men on the front lines, where they rightfully belonged, and all that was left for us was one slice of corned beef and a cup of cold coffee for each meal. Once or twice we managed to get bread and cheese with our corned beef, and one time we even got a spoonful of apricot jam to spread over our cold, greasy canned beef. Even though such a combination sounds sickening now, at the time it was delicious.

After about a week's stay in Cherbourg we boarded trucks and traveled about 25 miles to the town of Carentan, France. I'll never forget that place, for it was the first real French town of any size that we had ever seen. I was rather shocked by the sidewalk urinals that appeared on nearly every corner but soon got used to them. It was also at Carentan that I saw my first "40 and 8" box cars, which are so named from the inscription on the side of the car reading "40 hommes - 8 chevaux" (40 men, 8 horses). The car measures 21 feet long and seven feet wide with sliding doors in the middle on both sides. You can imagine how cramped we were when they loaded 40 of us with all our luggage and rations in one car that afternoon.

Traveling in one of those "40 and 8's" was an adventure in itself; for at the time, the present synchronized railroad schedules had not been established. When the train left, the engineer had no idea what time he would reach his destination. In fact, most of the time he didn't know over what tracks he would travel, which made the ride most interesting. Not knowing how long the trip would last, we had to carry enough "C" rations with us to last a week just in case it required longer than the three days it took us. Personnel were not considered top priority at that time, so we would have to side-track every hour or so and let a red-ball supply train by. When these stops were made we would all jump out of the car and start hunting for apples, cider, bread, and cheese. Apple orchards crowded the

5

right-of-way, so it was not any trouble to obtain them, but the other items had to be bought from the French civilians in their farmhouses and villages.

At night we would try to sleep anywhere we could find room, which was usually on top of someone else. It was rather cold for that time of year, and the combination of rain and wind leaking in the car just about froze us. We would bundle up in our overcoats and field jackets and sit up in a corner somewhere. After about ten minutes you would find someone sitting on your leg, so you would ask him to move. A few minutes later someone else would ask you to move, so we never did get more than a half-hour's sleep at a time during the entire trip.

Finally, we arrived at our destination just outside of Le Mans, France, the 14th Replacement Depot. There we also slept in the field in pup tents, but at least we had good meals, served in a field kitchen. Naturally we were put on the alert as soon as we arrived there and couldn't get any passes. Our stay only lasted about three days at Le Mans, and we again boarded "40 and 8's."

After another three-day train ride, we arrived at Neufchateau, France. Some old French cavalry school barracks provided sleeping quarters for us there; but naturally, we replacements had to sleep on the floor in the attic loft. Here, too, we were constantly being called out for training marches, inspections, etc., so it was a great relief to be alerted for shipment after a week's stay. We had several final clothing checks, for we knew by then that we were in Patton's Third Army and would probably go directly to an outfit. Finally, the night of departure, we loaded all our equipment on our backs and fell out of the barracks to board the trucks. We all lined up for a last-minute roll call, and to my surprise the sergeant called out "Private James A. Cutter, 37636627, deleted. Return to your barracks." I couldn't for the life of me figure out why I should be taken off shipment, but I didn't object at all.

There were five of us removed from the packet and held there at the 17th Replacement Depot. Two of the men, S/Sgt. Bill Jaffe and Pvt. John Auernhammer, were deleted because they could speak German and were needed as linguists. Another fellow, Pvt. Devereaux, had suffered an attack of pneumonia and was still running a high fever. The last fellow, Cpl. Creech (the non-com with our lost baggage detail in Cherbourg), was the only man in the packet who had a heavy machine gunner's MOS (Military Occupational Specialty) number. Everyone had a reason for being held over except me, and none of us could figure out why I had been deleted. We were allowed to move into a private room downstairs in the same building, and since it had an improvised stove and an electric light, we couldn't complain any. Another good feature about the place was the fact that we could have passes to town, and it was there I had my first opportunity to exercise my small French vocabulary.

The first pass Auernhammer and I had was spent in buying all the French bread and cheese we could talk the people out of. We finally discovered that money meant nothing to the people, but for a pack of cigarettes or a chocolate bar you could buy practically anything.

The second time we went to town we took Jaffe along, for we had heard that there was a restaurant there that served steak dinners (even though a court martial was threatened to anyone caught eating at a French establishment). We went to the place we had been told about and found it was just another cafe with no food served at all. We were just about to give up when Jaffe discovered a civilian who could speak German, so he asked if there was any place in town that served steak. He directed us to a small cafe way out on the edge of town in a section that was out of the way for GIs. Sure enough, we went there and had one of the most delicious steak dinners I have ever had. The first night we had potato soup and brown bread with our steaks, but the next night we were treated to a side dish of French fries in addition to the rest. The cafe reminded me of something out of a movie I had seen, for every night a beautiful, redheaded French girl paratrooper would visit there with a captain escort. Several times she had a friend along who would play the piano for us if we coaxed her enough.

For the first time in France, I really enjoyed myself there at Neufchateau. At first, they had me doing all sorts of miscellaneous details such as cleaning out buildings and digging trenches, but after a while they had me working as assistant clerk in the orderly room. That all came to an end, though, when I was alerted for shipment after two weeks.

Up until the time for shipment I still didn't know why I was being held over. As soon as my shipping order came out, though, I finally discovered the reason. Someone had looked over my service record, had seen I used to be a photographer, and transferred me from the infantry to the 166th Signal Photo Lab. In other words, at last I was out of the infantry! I was so happy I couldn't wait to write the news home! I was to be shipped to the 38th Replacement Battalion and from there to the 166th Signal Battalion with the signal corps.

Finally, one rainy night, I said goodbye to my three remaining comrades (Cpl. Creech had shipped out about a week earlier) and took off by truck for the 38th at Toule. I didn't mind the rain: I didn't mind anything. I was so happy at getting out of the infantry! I didn't even mind when they put me on KP (Kitchen Police, or dishwasher) at the 38th, for I was sure it wouldn't last for long. I had seen my orders, and I was definitely in the signal corps!

I met Creech again at Toule and learned from him that most of the other men from our replacement packet had been there and gone on to the 26th Infantry Division. The 38th depot also supplied men to the 35th, the 80th, and the 90th Infantry Divisions and to the 4th Armored Division and 6th Armored Division as well as some special attached organizations.

I spent a very joyous (but rainy) Thanksgiving Day there at Toule - happy with the thoughts that I would soon be completely divorced from the infantry. However, the next morning at 1030 I was told to pack my things and be ready to leave at 1000 to join the 26th Infantry Division. Realizing there must be some mistake, I dashed over to the orderly room and tried to appeal my case. The only answer I could get from them was, "I don't care where the heck you were assigned at the last station! You go wherever we send you!" Realizing that I was supposed to have been ready a half hour before, I quickly threw my equipment in my bag and climbed on the truck.

Needless to say, my heart was in my mouth; and I was actually too scared to be disappointed for long. I knew that this was one of the last steps towards combat; for that day, November 24, 1944, I joined the 26th, "Yankee" Division. First, we were taken to division headquarters at Nancy and from there quickly shuttled to the 104th Regimental Service Company, which was set up in a stable at the time. However, the next day it was moved to Nebing, France, and set up on the second floor of a contractor's lumber shack.

On the 27th of November I was assigned to Company B (also called Baker Company), the organization with which I was to remain for seven months of combat. It was wonderful to be assigned to a company at last; and the welcome that we, as new replacements, were given was really heartfelt. We had been used to the kicking around in replacement depots for so long we had forgotten how decent, human treatment felt. It was really swell when the first sergeant, James Cortez, came out of the CP (Command Post) with outstretched hand to greet each one of us. Then he asked if there was anything he could do, if there was anything we needed in the way of PX supplies or equipment. We couldn't get used to the sudden change, and I have never lost the great admiration for Cortez that I gained that day.

At the time we joined the company they had a total strength of 18 men instead of the 187 men they should have. There were 12 of us replacements, and Cortez let us pick any job in the platoons we wanted. My favorite weapon in the infantry is the 60mm. mortar, so I chose to be in a mortar squad. Well, I asked for it, so they made me an ammo bearer and threw me 48 pounds of ammunition to carry in addition to my rifle and pack!

We stayed around Nebing - eating, sleeping, and enjoying the rest most of the time - until the 29th, when we moved to Grening. We started practicing together as organized teams and finally went into combat on December 1.

Level	Unit	Commander/Leader	Approx. Size
Infantry Division	26th Infantry Division (Yankee Division)	Maj. Gen. Willard S. Paul	15,000
Infantry Regimen	104th Infantry Regiment	Col. Ralph A. Palladino	3,000–3,200
Infantry Battalion	1st Battalion	Lt. Col. Leon Gladding Maj. Amarita	850–900
Rifle Company	Company B	Capt. Stout	150–200
Rifle Platoon	1st Platoon	Lt. Schmutz	40–45

Organizational chart showing James's position in the 1st Platoon of Company B during World War II. Although the ideal unit size is listed here, it was rarely maintained in the later months of the war—as James noted, his Company B at this point comprised only 18 men and 12 replacements.

CHAPTER II

Coming up through the replacement depots, I had heard wounded men on their way back up to duty tell weird, almost unbelievable stories about combat. On the boat crossing the channel I had seen men bearing gruesome scars on their way back to the lines, and their tales would frighten even the toughest replacements. So, you can see I wasn't too anxious to go into combat. However, by the time we were ready to go on line I had made many friends in the company, especially with the replacements who had entered with me. I remember one fellow named Stock really well, for he had been a photographer too. He was a Jewish fellow but not at all the obnoxious Brooklyn type in his ways. In fact, he was the other way around; and after you spent a few hours with him you knew all his personal life and history. He was exceptionally friendly, and I learned that his wife was still living in Washington, where he had previously worked for the Government photographing maps. His favorite weapon was the machine gun, so he volunteered to be a machine gunner.

Dobrinski was another gunner who was a special friend of mine. He is a Russian fellow and sports a mustache exactly like Joseph Stalin. He is a quiet guy, but you can't help but like him for his efficient manner. Another close friend back there was Crystophiac, who was my squad leader at the time. His wife is an air-wac (woman's army corps) and both are nuts about airplanes. He is a licensed pilot for small non-commercial planes.

I'll never forget my first real day of combat and baptism to enemy fire. We started the day off in a woods on top of a high hill just outside of Saare-Union. Artillery had been pounding the town for 24 hours, and another outfit was supposed to have taken the town. Our orders were to go by the left side of the town and secure the woods on the far side. If we had been told our objective before the push-off, I wouldn't have been quite so frightened; but as it was, no one knew just what to expect so we were all scared: old timers and new men alike. After an hour of hiking with my extra 48-pound burden, though, I was more tired than scared.

We were walking beside a railroad track in the usual single file formation with five yards between each man when I received my first shock. No one was talking, everything was quiet when I happened to glance to the side of the road and see a German lying there with a terrifying death stare on his face. In the small of his back was a tie which supported him in such a way that his mouth hung open and his eyes popped wide open. About 20 yards down the road I saw my first dead American, but some thoughtful GI had turned him over on his stomach, so his face was hidden. Those were the first two dead I saw, and after that death did not bother me.

We passed on by the two corpses and followed the railroad tracks on down. Thus far everything had been quiet, so we were not overly cautious. I was near the end of the column, so I felt comparatively safe. We came to one spot where we had to climb up an embankment, cross the tracks, and go down on the other side. The end of the column had just completed this maneuver when I heard my first German shell at close range. It was an 88mm. cannon throwing direct fire at us, and it exploded on the tracks just above my head. I didn't know what it was at first, so I just flattened out on the ground and waited. Another explosion came just above our heads, and I knew another one had landed. Just then I heard a sharp popping noise overhead and learned that a burp gun had opened up on us. (Several models of the German machine pistols and machine guns are called "burp guns" because they fire at such a rapid rate it sounds like "burp.") I was really getting the works that day, for the Krauts (Germans) used just about every weapon they had. The next 88 to land broke behind us in a field about 15 yards away. All the old timers just kept lying flat on the ground, so I followed suit and tried to bury myself into the earth. Finally, Captain Stout said it was time to move out, so we advanced up the tracks.

That afternoon I started to dig my first foxhole in combat. We were still by the railroad embankment, so we felt fairly safe from enemy shell fire. I had just about completed my hole when the order came to move out. This time we crossed the tracks again, walked about 100 yards across an open field without receiving any fire, and entered the woods. We saw several casualties there but proceeded up to the front of the woods and started digging in again for the night.

It was still raining, and as darkness closed in all hell broke loose! 88's started falling in on us almost as heavily as the rain, and every one of them was a tree burst, which showered shrapnel throughout the woods. After dodging them for five or ten minutes we decided that we would never finish our foxhole, so we stood up and continued digging. Finally, one came too close and burst in the tree almost directly overhead. I felt a sharp sting in my back, and when I reached my hand back there, I found a big hole torn out of my raincoat. There was no blood, though, so we kept on digging. Finally, the hole was finished and had only soaked up eight inches of water, so we climbed in and pulled the shelter half over us. We were dead tired, so we fell asleep just as soon as we hit bottom.

That evening about ten o'clock I heard someone calling my name. I opened my eyes, but I might just as well keep them closed for all the good it did on that black night. It was still pouring rain as hard as before, so I was really disgusted when the squad leader told us to grab whatever we could and follow him. We weren't sure what was happening; but we could hear tanks moving around in the distance, so we didn't hesitate. We grabbed our packs, ammo and rifles and ran with him to the company CP, where all the men were assembling. Just as we got there a machine gun started spraying the woods with tracers from behind us! Needless to say, I didn't like the looks of things, so I was only too glad to move out, which we did just as soon as we rounded up as much of the company as we could. We finally withdrew with about 3/4ths. of the company and the German tanks only 25 yards away.

We stumbled and felt our way back to our starting positions of that morning and climbed into our old holes, which were now about half full of water. Later that night Sgt. Meldanado, platoon sergeant, (we only had one good-size platoon for a company) came in leading the rest of the company, so we didn't lose any men by the Jerry (German) counterattack. I later learned that our orders to withdraw had come before the counterattack, for some other outfit was supposed to be on our right flank. They had not accomplished their mission of the day, so we had been left dangerously out on our own.

We spent the next day trying to dry out our clothing. When I awoke that morning, I found all but my head completely submerged in water and my pockets floating at my side. So, I really needed to dry all over. The cooks brought up two hot meals that day, so we felt much better. We also received more replacements that day and I was surprised to find Devereaux, the fellow who had pneumonia back at the replacement depot, among them. We had a good old reunion until we had to jump off on the attack that night.

We walked until midnight and then were really relieved when we pulled up at an old German sanitarium and were told we could sleep there that night. Believe me, I didn't need a second invitation and I was stretched out on a table and fast asleep before I knew what had happened.

The next morning, we jumped off early and went into the attack just as it was getting light. That day we walked about fifteen miles and didn't receive any enemy fire at all. In fact, the only trace of Krauts we found was when we passed a spot where our artillery had blown up an ammo (ammunition) truck. All the trees near-by were damaged and filled with parts of German bodies and clothing. The only bad part about the whole scene was one hand with part of a GI shirt cuff clinging to it, which we saw about 25 yards away from the scene. The only explanation we could find for that was that perhaps some GI the Jerries had taken prisoner was riding on the ammo truck when it was hit.

Our orders called for us to relieve the 101st Infantry Regiment that night, and we were too tired to move another step. My feet were terribly blistered, and I felt like I just couldn't move. It was still pouring down rain and it looked like another night out in a foxhole. We were all dreading it so much I think we would have done anything to get out of going on. One kid was so desperate he fell out of the column while going through a town, grabbed an ax, and chopped off one of his fingers to keep from going on! Captain Stout didn't want to go on any more than we did, but he had to or be court martialed. Finally, he conveniently got lost right outside of an old Jerry camp, so we had to go in the basement and sleep there all night.

When I awoke the next morning, I felt a little better, but my feet were still in very bad condition. They were all swollen and blistered so badly I had to change socks every time we stopped for a while. Several times my feet were so swollen I had to fight to get the shoes back on again. I found a good way to dry socks is to wear them around your waist next to your underwear, so every day I had dry socks to put on.

We started out on the attack again that day, December 6, and one of the first things we had to do was wade through a creek with about two feet of water in it. There went my feet again! However, we continued on up to the top of the next hill and took a break. It was just as we were resting that things started to pop. First a burp gun opened up followed by numerous small arms fire. The first burst killed one of our men, but a German SS (Storm Trooper) fell in return for it. After a while peace was restored with all the Krauts driven out of the woods, so we started digging in.

That night the fellow I was sleeping with and I decided we had better keep one man in our hole awake all night, so we took shifts sitting up in the hole and doing guard. Around midnight I heard several shots, then a hand grenade, and then several more shots. The sound came from the edge of the woods (about 15 yards away) and at a place where we had one of our light machine guns located. We sent an aid man up, and the next morning

I found that Stock, one of my best friends, had been killed. He had noticed some men out in front of his foxhole and had made the mistake of challenging them instead of shooting. They tossed a hand grenade into his hole and killed him. Then they turned and fled.

The following afternoon we were sitting around eating our "C" rations when someone reported Heinies (Germans) in the other end of the woods, where they had been the preceding day. Our orders were to drop everything, grab our rifles, and run; and that is exactly what we did. We shot our way through the woods, killing several Germans after they had wounded one or two of our boys, and then built up a defense line on the far edge. From there we could see a German pillbox on the opposite hill.

Just about that time, our artillery started firing and landing short. It landed right in the middle of our men and produced several casualties including one man killed. We radioed back to cease firing, but it kept on coming for a few minutes, adding several more casualties. I sweated out that barrage all right and was preparing to eat a little supper when our artillery started falling short again. At the time I was standing next to our weapons platoon sergeant, Sgt. Hoag, and another man. We were holding empty "C" ration cans up against a tree to catch rainwater for drinking, when one of the shells hit and exploded in the same tree! I fell to the ground, but just when my head got about a foot from the earth a large piece of shrapnel landed right where my head was to be and splashed mud up in my face. I felt all over myself to see if I was covered with mud or blood, decided it was mostly the former, and got up to help the two men I was standing with at the time. Both of them were badly wounded - Sgt. Hoag in the left leg and the other fellow in the right arm. I took my sling from my carbine to use as a tourniquet on the one man's arm while Captain Stout helped Hoag. Finally, an aid man came up and dressed both of their wounds, so Meldanado, Barret (another mortar man), and I helped carry them back to the battalion aid station.

We couldn't find our first battalion station, so we dropped him off at the third. While there, we decided we would try to get something to put on our feet, so we took off our shoes for the doctor to look at them. He told us we all three had trench foot and sent us back to the hospital. That was December 7, 1944 - three years after Pearl Harbor.

I'll never forget how wonderfully we were treated back at the 114th Medical Battalion (clearing station) or how wonderful it was just to be able to lie down on a cot again. Just to be able to shave and wash my face was worth a million dollars and eating hot chow (food) was just like heaven. I couldn't get used to the peace and quiet back there in the hospital or how swell the medics treated us. We had to leave our feet out from under the covers and bathe them every hour with alcohol to get them toughened up again.

While back at the 114th Medical Battalion we heard rumors that we were to be relieved by the 87th Infantry Division, but we couldn't believe it was true until we returned to our regimental service company on the 10th and saw them starting to come up. Sure enough, our division was being relieved as soon as it crossed the German border (just east of Kalhausen, France), our division objective. Then we were supposed to have anywhere from 30 days to three months rest in Metz, France. Fortunately, we timed things just right and didn't have to return to the companies until they were in Metz; for when I rejoined the outfit there were exactly 12 men left out of the 60 we had started out with just ten days earlier at Saare Union.

CHAPTER III

Rest at Metz was just a taste of basic training all over again with all of the disadvantages and few of the advantages. We were very grateful to be quartered in buildings again with separate rooms for each platoon. We were even able to find a small stove to provide heat, and after scraping around a while managed to find enough beds and straw mattresses for everyone. It was a disappointment to find no electricity in the power lines, though, for the only way we could provide light at night was to burn grease in open tin cans. We didn't feel too inconvenienced with the lack of electricity, water, central heating, etc., for the combat time we had put in made us all thankful for whatever little comforts we did have.

When our division moved into Metz, the city had not been entirely taken from the enemy; and the 101st Infantry Regiment had to enter the city several days before the rest of us came off the line in order to clean out the last remaining fort. The surrounded Germans quickly surrendered however, so we were free from all noises of combat during our rest period, save for the noise of our own men out on the practice ranges. We were very much surprised to find ourselves standing reveille the first morning after arriving in Metz and were twice as surprised to find ourselves doing close order drill and physical exercises right after breakfast. Several of us protested, "This was supposed to be a rest!" but soon learned that a training schedule had been laid out by higher headquarters for our entire stay there.

The next day we were marched at attention out to a German rifle range and given the opportunity to "zero in" our weapons! We, who had just come out of combat where our very lives depended upon the accuracy of our pieces, were given lessons in how to load, sight, and fire the M1 rifle! That was too much! Right then and there I decided I would become a professional goldbrick (goof off)!

There was one really good feature about Metz, though, and that was the wonderful meals we ate there. In all my time overseas, I have never seen meals to equal those. I understand the reason for such excellent quality was because the mess sergeant was drawing enough food for a full company (187 men) and just feeding our handful of men. At any rate, it wasn't unusual to sit down to a mess kit full of four or five different kinds of vegetables, two varieties of meat (usually steak or chicken), and at least two different kinds of desserts (with pies or pastries of some kind included). We certainly made gluttons of ourselves, but we were surprised at the small capacity we were able to hold. The continual diet of "K" and "C" rations had shrunk our stomachs! I was never able to pin the blame directly on the food or the water, but during my entire stay at Metz I suffered from chronic and completely involuntary diarrhea. I wasn't alone in my suffering, however, for Captain Stout spent his entire rest period in bed with the same ailment.

At the end of the first week in rest we heard of a new campaign the Germans had launched in the Ardennes. At the same time our company started receiving replacements by the truck loads, so we all suspected something was up. Sure enough, on the evening of December 19, our company was brought up to full strength and we were alerted. Being one of the few non-coms in the group (I received my promotion from buck private to buck sergeant on the 17th), I was expected to help organize the unit into a fighting outfit. Two other non-coms, Sgt. Dobrinski and Sgt. Carmen (both of whom were promoted at the same time I was), and I worked with the first sergeant all night attempting to get each man fully equipped with all his weapons, ammunition, and pack articles. The whole thing was a great nightmare of confusion because all of the men were new to the infantry and hadn't received one day's training when they were transferred from the artillery, anti-aircraft, ordnance, signal corps, etc. To top it all off, none of the men knew what platoon they belonged to or what their specific job was.

Finally, at six o'clock the next morning, our company was assembled in the pitch black of early morning and loaded onto five large trailer vans. It was then I discovered a fortunate "break" for me: during the confusion of the night, Captain Stout, while organizing the company, had forgotten my new rating and had made me a company runner. I call that a break, for the job of runner is at times much safer than that of squad leader in the infantry, and by the time the error was detected, it was too late to make any changes.

And so, we left Metz, our rest area, which we had hoped would at least last until Christmas. But as fate would have it, we had to return to the lines and spend Christmas in a foxhole.

CHAPTER IV

Everything had been fine and dandy until (German General) Von Rundstedt started that winter push through Belgium and Luxembourg, later known as the Battle of the Ardennes and commonly called "the Bulge." We were really beginning to enjoy ourselves at Metz when we were so quickly whisked away into combat again.

We arrived in Luxembourg that evening and hiked to a large forest where we dug-in and bivouacked. Luckily the weather was foggy all that day, or I feel sure we would have been made targets by the German air corps the way we rode those trucks. The next day the division reconnaissance unit was sent out to contact the enemy (at that time no one knew just how far the bulge had progressed), and the following morning at 3:00 A.M. we moved into the attack during our first snowstorm in Luxembourg. That morning we hiked 18 miles with full field equipment over some of the worst terrain I had seen. My hands were just about frozen, and my clothes froze to me after being soaked by the wet snow.

We were further alarmed when gas masks were issued to all of us, and we were told if the enemy intended to use gas during the war, now would be the most logical time. I don't need to explain the effect that freezing cold weather had upon the soft rubber of the masks except to say that not one mask in the entire company fit! The rubber was frozen and had become stiff and brittle. Besides, in order to wear my face piece, I was forced to remove my glasses, which made me practically useless as a fighting man. All we could do was hope and pray the Krauts would decide not to gas us, for our masks were absolutely useless.

We finally reached our positions that night and dug-in without a shot having been fired. Then came the heart-breaking but always expected news. We had just finished a beautiful foxhole and made up a nice warm bed when orders came to move out. We rolled our equipment and pulled out, making perfect silhouette targets with a bright moon against a foot of snow. It was rather rough cross-country hiking, and we were uneasy when we found out the Germans were wearing all white snow suits. We walked about two hours, failed to locate the unit we were supposed to, and returned to our holes. All we had seen was a German patrol car (which turned around and fled) and around two dozen prisoners another outfit had captured. I finally crawled into bed and got three hours of sleep before we received orders to move out on the attack at 0300.

Again, we hiked for three hours through woods and mountains. By that time my feet were swollen and completely numb at a time when they should have been warm from walking. Remembering how the doctor had told me to get on sick call the first time I noticed trench foot returning, I told the sergeant about it and left the company when we reached the next town. That was December 23, and we still hadn't fired a shot.

I was treated at our first battalion aid station, but through transportation mix-up I was returned to the third battalion of the 328th Infantry Regiment. There my feet were again examined, and I was sent back to the 114th Medical Battalion Clearing Station. I stayed there overnight and was returned to our regimental service company in time to spend Christmas Eve with them. The next day, Christmas, I discovered I was scheduled to be returned to the company at 1400 (2 p.m. Military time starts at midnight - 0000 - and counts up for 24 hours) with the big turkey dinner scheduled for 1600. I thought I would miss Christmas dinner for sure until I found the 101st Infantry Regiment's Collecting Company Kitchen. They were eating at noon and invited me to share their dinner, which I gladly did.

When I rejoined the company Christmas night, they were just fighting their way into Eschdorf, and after a furious tank battle we entered and occupied a three-quarters destroyed farm house on the far edge of town. The troops were dug-in on the outside of town to protect it while the battalion moved its CP into the better homes in the center of town. One thing I saw in that town I will never forget. Right next to our company CP building was a small shrine with a crucifix in it. Parked behind that small building was a huge German tank which had been almost completely destroyed and burned out during the fierce battle; but the little shrine had not been touched at all. The monstrous German vehicle was almost touching that fragile structure, but the crucifix and iron grilled door remained as beautiful as ever while the tank smoldered behind it.

I remember the next day in Eschdorf eight of us were resting up against a building alongside the road when two planes flew fairly low overhead. Never having been bothered by the Luftwaffe (air force) in France, I didn't pay any attention to them until I heard what sounded like a string of firecrackers going off and saw the concrete being chipped off the wall just a few feet above my head. I really hit the dirt in a hurry and started crawling under a wagon. Then the second plane roared down and sprayed us with lead. Fortunately, they didn't hit anyone, but by the time they circled for a second try we were all inside buildings, and the place looked deserted. About five minutes later we had the pleasure of seeing those two planes knocked out by our own ack-ack (anti-aircraft) units.

That same day three more German planes came over and started strafing just as we were eating noon chow. I ducked into the potato cellar of the house with one of the company medics, Bob Getsfred. We started talking about the medics and he mentioned the shortage of aid men. Since I had been trying to get into the medical corps ever since I joined the army, I jumped at the opportunity. That afternoon he took me down to see the battalion surgeon, Captain Winestock, who told me they could use me and would arrange for the transfer. I was to return to the company and wait for further notice from him. Incidentally, some of our own P-47 fighter planes showed up that day and shot down all three of the Krauts with the help of our own ack-ack.

During the strafing another amusing incident occurred to the other company medic, Nagurney. "Nag" is six feet six inches tall and just about as awkward at times as he is long. He dove into a roofless building during the strafing and was hugging as close to the ground as possible. Bullets were popping all around, so even after the shooting stopped he held his position for several seconds. Finally, when he thought all was clear, he started to stand up when he heard a sharp ping right beside him. He immediately dropped to the ground there and refused to move for five minutes. When he finally investigated the source of the noise he discovered it had been caused by a 50-caliber metal clip (such as is used to hold airplane ammo together), which had taken that long to fall to the earth.

The next evening, we moved out again and hiked about 10 more miles against a heavy snow with a brilliant moon. Luckily, we only ran into one sniper that night, and he missed as he fired his last shots. We finally dug-in (try digging in frozen ground through a foot of snow with a small hand shovel sometime - it's fun!) around midnight on the edge of the burning town of Kaundorf, Luxembourg, about six miles southeast of Wiltz.

Dad's foxhole buddy William Fairfield, decorated by Leon Gladding

Three members of the 104th Infantry Regiment, 26th Division, are cited by Maj. Leon Gladding, Springfield, Mass.; L to R: Sgt. William Farsfield, Skowhegan, Maine, awarded the Silver Star for gallantry in action; T/5 Oce Trueblood, Vandallia, Ill., awarded the Bronze Star for meritorious service beyond the line of duty; T/4 Matthew Buda, Springfield, Mass., also awarded the Bronze Star for meritorious service beyond the line of duty. With Major Gladding is Lt. Carl Croce, Skowhegan, Maine at Eschdorf, Luxembourg. 27 Dec 1944. Signal Corps # SC 324555.
Photo by U.S. Army Signal Corps; caption by U.S. Army Signal Corps

Addendum caption by Gary Cutter; A month before my father James Cutter passed at age 90, I showed him this photograph. James immediately recognized his old foxhole buddy William Fairfield, noting that the Signal Corps caption misspelled his name as "Farsfield."

17

Standing in history's footsteps – Eschdorf, Luxembourg 2016

In March 2016, I travelled to Eschdorf. With the help of local amateur historian Fred Fey, we found the exact location where the U.S. Army Signal Corps photographed the 1944 decoration of three soldiers from the 104th Infantry Regiment. This photo was taken from the same spot, more than 70 years later.
Photo by Gary Cutter; caption by Gary Cutter

2016 Visit to Eschdorf – locating the shrine untouched by war

Fred Fey, a local historian, helped search the streets of Eschdorf to find the shrine my father described in his wartime account. Though the town has more than one small shrine, only one features an iron grilled door—matching the scene he remembered: a crucifix untouched beside a smoldering German tank. More than 70 years later, the shrine still stands.
Photo by Gary Cutter; caption by Gary Cutter

Soldiers in Company B (James's company), showing freezing conditions

Pvt. Lloyd Spencer, Portland, ORE. and Pvt. James Bryson, Lynn, Mass. Take a well earned rest in the woods they fought in, near Wiltz, Luxembourg. Both men are with B Company, 104th Infantry Regiment. 26th Division. January 6, 1945
Photo by U.S. Army Signal Corps; caption by U.S. Army Signal Corps

Getting up at daybreak the next day, we shoved off through the thickest pine woods, heaviest snow, and steepest hills I had yet seen. For five solid hours we pushed along, trying to make a path through the heavy woods. We didn't take the roads because it would expose us too much, but finally that afternoon we decided we would have to. After only ten minutes on the road we ran into trouble. I was up front, and we were just rounding a sharp turn when we heard a tank coming. It was so close we didn't have time to run for cover, so we froze on the road and radioed the rear of the column to take for the woods. As the tank rounded the bend he ran squarely into us with guns pointed right at us. We were helpless, for our small arms would bounce off its sides; and we were like fish in a barrel for its machine guns. Also, that long 88mm. cannon on the front of the tank looked as big as a 16-inch coast gun as it pointed right at my head. We must have looked pretty determined, though, for it came to an abrupt stop and four German heads popped out shouting "Kamerad! Kamerad!" So, we stripped them of souvenirs put the driver back inside the tank (which was carrying a full load of ammunition) with a GI guard and drove the tank back to town with the three other Germans marching in front of it with their hands clasped on top of their heads. I would give anything for a picture of that - those "supermen" were really a miserable sight to see.

By that time the battalion CO (Commanding Officer) decided we had gotten far enough, for we were out on our own at least two miles ahead of any support in an area which we later found was thick with Jerries. We dug-in for the night; but you guessed it - we didn't sleep in those holes - at least not right away. Instead, we moved out to contact the company on our right. After hunting for over six hours in the dark we discovered they weren't in position where they should have been, so we pulled back to our old holes at about 4:00 AM. and tried to get some sleep. The next afternoon we moved out for an evening's adventure I'll never forget.

Our orders were to move to a position and tie in with the right flank of another company. Reconnaissance had shown that the woods we were to move through were cleared of Germans, but we soon found out differently. It was one of those still nights with a full moon, and we made perfect targets against the white snow. Besides, the Jerries were all wearing white snow capes, which are perfect camouflage at night. En-route to our new positions we passed several Nazi corpses and a good deal of German equipment, which didn't help to quiet our puzzled minds any. In other words, we were all jittery and "trigger happy." We all had our weapons fully loaded with the safety off even though we had been assured there was no trouble ahead. It was just one of those uneasy nights that you probably can't understand.

At any rate, we met the company we were to tie into (which relieved us some) and were cutting across an open field for the next patch of woods, which we were to occupy. Being the runner, I was the fourth or fifth man from the front of the line. Just as we got to within 25 yards of the woods a German machine gun opened up on us from the woods with direct, head-on fire. I felt the bullets brush by and instinctively fell flat on my face in the snow. Then I started feeling my body for blood, for I was positive they couldn't have missed me. Strangely enough, they hadn't hit me! After satisfying myself on this point I began to realize that those tracers were still grazing me and that I had better get out of there right away. I turned around and started burrowing back towards the woods we had just left. It was just like the infiltration course in basic training - only this time not in fun. I'll bet I scooped a couple of gallons of snow inside my shirt and coat, for I really kept flat on the ground. When I reached the edge of the woods I jumped up and ran in still farther, passing several German-dug foxholes. I was tempted to jump into one of them, but I remembered about booby traps just in time.

After the firing stopped an officer from the other company came around and warned us to stay on the edge of the woods as it was heavily mined. There I was in the middle of it, and I had to get out somehow. That's when I really began to sweat, for I couldn't back track out into the machine gun. Finally, I got up enough nerve to walk out, and luck was with me. I didn't hit a single mine! In fact, only one man in the entire company was wounded by the machine gun, but we were all split up and disorganized.

By that time, we were all mad, so we organized a patrol to clean out the machine gun nest. We thought there was just one lone gun in the woods, so we charged it and were driven out with two casualties. Giving up the idea of capturing the woods at night, we dug-in about 50 yards from it and spent a very uneasy night. All night long the company on our left received German counter-attacks and piled up about 60 dead Jerries in a few hours.

I was badly shaken up that evening when Sgt. Carmen (the fellow who received his promotion the same day I did), was killed by a direct hit from a mortar. He had been made

20

platoon sergeant of the first platoon and was out checking his men when the shell came in. Now do you see why I was glad they made me a runner instead of a squad leader?

The next morning a platoon of our tanks drove up to within 50 yards of the woods and blasted it with machine gun and cannon fire for over 30 minutes. We moved in right afterwards and found the woods contained a whole machine gun company of Germans - mostly dead - but we took about eight dazed prisoners. The picture in the Grapevine (unit newspaper) shows the bazooka (anti-tank rocket) man who ran out to try to stop the tanks. He didn't get very far.

YD *Grapevine*, January 20, 1945

The Yankee Division newspaper shows snowy conditions. James drew the arrow pointing to the location of his foxhole.
Caption by Gary Cutter

The woods was over 100 yards long, and I'm willing to bet there wasn't one tree in that whole woods that didn't have a shrapnel mark on it from the terrific shelling the tanks gave it. In the end shown in the picture (the end where my hole was) at least 50 of the trees were blown down or weakened so much they fell down in a few days. In fact, every time the wind blew another tree fell.

We found the whole woods full of equipment and foxholes, and there was every type of German machine gun imaginable there. The night before I had been sleeping just 20 yards from a German machine gun. It's a good thing we didn't know the size force they had in that woods or none of us would have slept!

The assistant radio man was the one who was wounded the night before, so I took over his job - the first infantry work I enjoyed at all. Sgt. Fairfield (Bill Fairfield, a real New Englander with Yankee accent to prove it, was our radio man) and I took over a German foxhole and enlarged it for our own use. Then we lined it with German blankets, covered ourselves with more German blankets, and threw a Jerry shelter half over our heads to keep the snow off. Then we settled down for a nice rest. All that afternoon and night they shelled us with mortars and 88's, and casualties were great. Nagurney, our only medic by that time, was kept busy all afternoon and night.

The woods we were in was a valuable piece of ground for either side to hold, since it was the highest hill in that entire sector and was a perfect observation point. We had artillery observers with us all the time, and they could zero-in shells on Wiltz from there.

We had hoped the Jerries would let up on shelling us after the first few days, but we received fire every day from December 30 (when we moved in) until January 21 (when we moved out). They wounded an average of over two men every day with quite a few men killed. In other words, it was rather hot up there! One morning Nagurney and I were lying in our hole when three mortar shells came within five feet of us. Then the fourth round landed right on the edge of our hole, knocking a can of water from the ledge into our laps. It was a dud!

On December 31, a runner came up and told me my transfer had come through and to report to the aid station immediately. I really considered him a God-send, for the two days I had spent up there were two days of living hell! Never in the entire war was I shelled so much or so often. It was really a relief to be able to return to living in the aid station at Kaundorf. I spent one week under the guidance of Captain Winestock, learning the army way of applying first aid and supplementing my knowledge of medicine I had gained in pre-med school. It was really interesting work and a wonderful rest for me to be able to live in a house for a change. We treated a daily average of 15 or 20 patients who were seriously wounded.

At that time the battalion chaplain, a Catholic priest, lived with us in the aid station. I remember one evening we got a fellow from B Company who was just about dead. He had been clipped on the head by a shell fragment and had passed into secondary shock. He was unconscious when they brought him in, so we started giving plasma right away. That seemed to snap him out of it, for he immediately came to and began talking to us. We dressed his wounds and then everyone left the room except me. I was talking to him when all of a sudden, I noticed he was turning white and had gone out again. I quickly grabbed for his pulse and found he had none. His respiration seemed to have stopped completely, so I called for the captain right away; and after injecting large doses of caffeine and adrenaline into him, the captain was able to bring him around. However, he was still on the border line and we were all working feverishly when I noticed the chaplain standing there. He examined the fellow's dog tags, saw he was a Catholic, and immediately started giving him last rites while I worked away with the plasma bottle. None of us thought the patient had much chance of living, but before he left the aid station he was drinking coffee and joking with us. Right then is when I began to realize what a worthwhile job the medics were doing, and I was glad I had changed.

During my week at the aid station we changed battalion surgeons. Captain Winestock was transferred to the 101st Engineers and was replaced by a short little Texan, 1st Lt. Lindsey, who was taken into the army just as soon as he finished medical school and nine months of internship.

After talking to Sgt. Curto, our medical section sergeant, I had things fixed up, so I could return to my old outfit, Company B. Returning back to the line after that wonderful week of rest and warm bed (on the floor) was one of the hardest things I have ever done. I had treated several patients who had shot themselves in the hand or foot to get out of the war, and I'll have to confess that at that time I didn't blame them. In fact, if I had a little less will power I might have done the same, but I just couldn't understand anyone maiming himself for life. I did return to the company, though, and I was glad to find that most of my best friends had managed to survive even though the company had been whittled down to half size. The outfit was still in the same old place on top of "Purple Heart Hill," our name for the position because of the large number of casualties we suffered.

After about a week in position the kitchen had become sufficiently organized to send up coffee and cake with the rations every day at noon. This became a daily treat to which we looked forward with pleasure. Our supply line was rather long with about a five-mile haul by jeep from town and a half-mile portage by foot from the end of the jeep trail across open terrain by our woods. As a result, the coffee was usually iced by the time we got it, but we soon learned the trick of heating it over a small fire in our foxholes.

There were three of us aid men occupying the same foxhole, but every third night we were allowed to return to the aid station for over-night rest. That meant that only two of us had to sleep in the hole at one time. Before we left we had our shelter fixed up, so it was completely safe from anything but a direct hit by a shell. We had the roof lined with logs, a Kraut shelter half, and several inches of dirt. It was not only waterproof and shell fragment proof, but with the addition of a German shelter half over the entrance it was completely blacked out at night.

Three men of the second platoon occupied the foxhole next to ours, so it was considerably larger. Sgt. Cauffield, the squad leader, was working on the hole one day and found that he needed something heavy to hold down the blackout flap he had constructed out of a Heinie shelter half. He started feeling around in the snow for something when his hand fell upon the partially hidden body of a German soldier. Deciding that was just what he needed, he rolled the stiff over and anchored the end of the shelter half under him. That frozen Kraut remained their "paper weight" for the rest of our stay on Purple Heart Hill.

Cauffield was especially friendly to us medics and used to bring our coffee and rations over to us every day. He was usually a very cautious guy when the shells started coming in, for he had been with the company since Metz and had worked his way up to his present job. One afternoon the usual noon ration crowd of ten or fifteen men had cleared away from the CP (much to my relief) and just a few of us were standing around having our daily bull session. Cauffield was relieving himself nearby when some mortar shells started creeping in on us. We all dove for our holes as usual, but Cauffield for some reason or other didn't bother to hurry.

I was in my hole for a minute or two when I heard one land just outside and not more than five feet away. I pricked my ears up to hear the usual call "Medic!", but when

23

it didn't come I supposed no one had been hit. After things had quieted down I decided everything was too still, so I stuck my head out. The first thing I saw was Cauffield lying over next to Fairfield's hole, but he looked completely undamaged from where I was. Nevertheless, I grabbed my aid kits and jumped out to see what was the matter. Fairfield called over, "Never mind, Cutter. There's nothing you can do." It was then I noticed the half of his head and face away from me had been completely removed by the shell, which had landed just a few feet away from him. The explosion had also driven a splinter of wood through a five-gallon water can and thrown the container and water into Cunningham's and Fairfield's hole, dazing both of them for a few seconds. (Pat Cunningham, a gung-ho young Irishman with traditional gift of blarney, had replaced me as assistant radio man after I became a medic.)

That only left two men in the hole next to ours, but we all tried to forget about Cauffield death as soon as possible. Another of the three occupants received a fractured leg from a sniper's bullet several days later and was sent back to the States for convalescence. The third fellow, a really carefree screw-ball by the name of Case, had his left leg blown off a month later by a mortar shell in Saarlautern. I mention these things just to show that somehow or other I really did lead a charmed life during the seven months of combat. Counting up all the fellows I have slept with in the same foxhole, I discovered that there is only one fellow who didn't get hit, and that fellow is Fairfield.

Several nights later another incident happened that seems rather unbelievable now. Every hour on the hour there would be a contact patrol of two men from our company go over to communicate with "Fox" company on our right flank, a distance of several hundred yards. This one night it was darker than the ace of spades with a heavy fog hanging close to the ground, when I heard mortar shells landing on the path that led between our two companies. I didn't think much about it until I heard someone whisper, "Medic!" just outside my hole. I stuck my head out and found two fellows from "Fox" Company standing there, one of them whispering, "I got hit in the shoe on my way over here by a mortar fragment. I don't think it's anything serious, but I'd like to have you look at it." I told him to climb in, blacked out the hole, and lit the candle for a look. Sure enough, there was a small hole where the piece of metal had torn his combat boot, and inside I found a piece of shrapnel about the size of a butter bean.

I told him how lucky he was that the leather had stopped the shrapnel and started patching it up when I noticed blood on the other side of his foot. Then I turned his leg around and saw a hole on the other side of his leg directly opposite the first hole! That meant the man had a fractured leg and had been walking around on it without knowing it! I asked him if it pained him much, and he just answered, "Naw!" I thought to myself maybe it didn't then, but it would pretty quick - especially if he found out what condition his leg was really in. So, I gave him a shot of morphine, bandaged up his leg, and told him he was lucky just to have a flesh wound. Then he put his boot back on and walked all the way down to the ration point where I had a jeep waiting for him. Funny thing, he never did complain of any pain. I'll bet he thought I was really a dumb cluck or awfully careless when he found out the truth. Oh well, we didn't have any litters, and I didn't want to carry him piggy back. I knew that if he could make it all the way up from Fox Company he could certainly walk down to the jeep without hurting himself.

Several nights later the colonel decided to straighten out the battalion lines a little, so he ordered our first platoon to go out and form a road block on the main road to Wiltz.

At that time Wiltz was considered one of the key cities of the German offensive for it is like the hub of a wheel with a great many supply routes branching out from it. We were to form the block after one of the other companies had passed by there cleaning out all the Krauts. It all sounded simple - too simple. As luck would have it Captain Stout chose me as the medic to accompany the patrol, and from the start I didn't like the looks of things. We had been double crossed by other companies too many other times. Captain Stout felt the same way about it, so he waited four hours after the scheduled time for starting in order to give the other company time to get ahead of us.

We finally started out through the hip-deep snow, cursing at every foxhole filled with snow that we would fall into. The moon was fairly bright, and we still had our dark OD uniforms while the Krauts still had their all white camouflage uniforms. I was stationed at the platoon CP, a couple hundred yards away from where the road block was to be, in order to set up a sort of mini-aid station for any casualties they might have. The rest of the men finally reached their destination, scaring up a couple of Krauts on the way, but they quickly ran.

Several of the men started digging into position when they discovered a German patrol out in front of them using some sort of surveying instrument. Some wise guy in the platoon hollered out, "Kommen sie hier!" (Come here!), the Jerries shot up two flares, and then all hell broke loose. The flares had been a signal to an 88 up on the hill, whose presence we soon discovered when it opened up with direct fire. Lt. Schmutz (our platoon leader, a cool-headed and unpretentious guy) soon realized the futility of the situation; for no Americans had been through that area, and we were only a platoon in strength. He ordered the platoon to withdraw, but on the way back we suffered two casualties. One fellow, who was shot through the head, died; and the other fellow was dragged along on a broken leg. We finally got the wounded man evacuated and settled down to a night's sleep just as day broke at 0800 in the morning.

Towards the end of the month our entire company was moved back to Kaundorf for a day's rest, so we could clean up and shave. Following that we returned to the line and relieved Fox company, the outfit which had been on our right flank. It was disappointing to see what kind of holes they left us, for none of them was over two feet deep with only a shelter half over the top. Luckily, we only spent two nights there, but I'll never forget that second night.

While we were on the day's rest at Kaundorf, we had received several green replacements fresh from the States. This one new guy named Quick was on a standing guard post in the middle of the CP area when one of the worst mortar barrages I have ever heard started coming in. They were all small 50mm. shells but so thick it was almost impossible to distinguish between each individual explosion.

Quick should have dived into his hole as soon as he heard the first one come in, but like a fool he just stayed out there until he got hit. Then he screamed and yelled "Medic!" so loud I thought he must have had his entire leg blown off. Remembering that one of the first rules of the medics is that you won't do anyone any good if you get yourself killed trying to get to a wounded man, I told him to crawl in my hole and shut up or he would give away our position. Those shells were landing right on top of us, and the concussion from several of them bounced us around in our hole. I still can't understand why he wasn't killed. However, as soon as the barrage let up a little I decided I would risk going out to see which one of his legs had been blown off - if not both legs and arms the way he was screaming. Was I disgusted with him to find he only had a little chest wound! I took him in the foxhole and patched him up by candle light. The wound wasn't serious, but I knew it could develop into pleurisy or even a sucking wound if he didn't get back to the aid station quickly.

I phoned for the medical jeep with a litter and started him back to the ration point on foot to save time. He said he didn't know the way, so I sent a runner to accompany him. Imagine my surprise when an hour later I found him back again! He told me they had gotten lost, but the runner later confided in me that Quick was afraid to wait by himself for the jeep.

I sent him back a second time to the ration point and again called the jeep. The next morning, I learned he had refused to wait a second time for the jeep and had started back when he ran into Lt. Stanchfield, the CO of Charlie Company. The lieutenant was on his way back to the battalion forward CP so Quick walked all the way back with him - a distance of over three miles. I also learned that when he reached the aid station his condition was diagnosed as serious even though he had been only slightly wounded in action at first.

Fortunately, we pulled back to Kaundorf the next day after being relieved by the sixth cavalry. Spending a day there, we moved back still further for a three-day rest in Baschleiden, Luxembourg, and then returned to Noertrange, a small town just overlooking Wiltz, for another few days. I'll never forget the room I slept in there. It had only three walls, the fourth having been blown out by our own artillery during the period of occupation by the Germans. One old woman told us how several German staff officers had been standing in her kitchen shaving when an artillery shell came in through the window and, "Pft! Alles kaput!" (Utterly destroyed!).

From Noertrange we loaded on a truck and passed through Wiltz on our way back to France. I'll never forget one gruesomely funny sight en-route. A German soldier had been killed and had frozen with his hand to his head in a form of military salute. Some GI joker had propped him up so that everyone entering or leaving Wiltz was saluted by a bloody, icy corpse standing by the roadside!

CHAPTER V

Luxembourg had been a place of suffering for all of us. The cold had been intense, and we could never stand to be out of our foxholes for more than five minutes at a time; for if we were, we knew our feet would ache and throb for twelve hours afterwards. Yes, in spite of its beauty and grateful residents, Luxembourg was a miserable place; so, it was with no regret that we left the petite little country for lands unknown.

It goes without saying that our trip on the open trucks with the biting wind ripping through our clothing was anything but enjoyable. It was an all-day ride, so to pass the time more quickly we joked about what our post-war civilian plans were. "Tex" Woodward told about how he was going to dig a foxhole out in his back yard to sleep in and booby-trap his pants pockets at night to keep his wife out of them. I added that if a car ever backfired near me I would probably fall flat on my face in the nearest gutter and start digging in with my hat.

We continued our discussion along this ridiculous line until the subject gradually shifted to our prewar occupations. It finally came out that Tex was making over a million dollars a year on his trucking business, which he had leased to the army while he was in service. He was worried about paying his income tax when he was discharged because the last one had amounted to well over 150,000 dollars! He seemed like any other likable, good-natured Texan, and I couldn't believe he was a millionaire until one of the boys who had known him a long time verified the fact. His gift to his wife on her last birthday had been a Packard convertible, which she added to the family collection of cars.

Even though I had only known Tex for a few weeks we became the best of friends, and he swore that just as soon as I finished medical school I would become his personal physician. "But, Tex," I protested, "I'm probably going to live in St. Louis, and San Antonio is a long way from there!" In all seriousness he assured me that it didn't make any difference and he would either come up to see me or pay my way down to visit him.

"I want you to come down and visit me just as soon as the war is over anyway; and by golly, if you don't, I'm going to come up to St. Louis and get you!" he would declare in his slow Texas drawl. At first, I thought he was only kidding about my visiting him, but during the next few weeks I found out he was really serious. So, I was looking forward to an enjoyable visit after the war.

During one of our intimate discussions later on I learned that he had served three years in the army before and had received a blue discharge (one "without honor"). That was his reason for re-enlisting in this war - so he could receive a white discharge to erase the former black mark on his service record. I've forgotten the reason why he didn't receive a white discharge the first time, but it had something to do with some member of his family being sick, so he went AWOL (Absent Without Leave) to get home after he tried without results to obtain a furlough. The one thing I do remember is that he had gotten a raw deal and was so anxious to go through life with a clean record that he had re-enlisted even though he could have stayed out the entire war.

That evening, after the all-day trip from Noertrange, we arrived at a small town just on the edge of the Maginot Line, France's ill-fated defensive system, which had been much more elaborate than Germany's Siegfried Line. We de-trucked and started walking towards our destination, Pikard, Germany. We were very pleased to notice that the snow in that area was nowhere near as deep or as cold as it had been in Luxembourg. Not knowing just what to expect, we shied at the many rows of silent pillboxes along the route and finally pulled into our small town to pick out a house for the night. About two miles east of us we could see white-phosphorus shells bursting and showering their beautiful, but death dealing, red sparks just like some colossal Fourth of July celebration. We knew we were very close to the front lines, for we could hear the roar of our own artillery behind us. By that time, I was too tired and too cold to worry about such an insignificant thing as the war, so I heated up a cup of soluble coffee and a ration and went to bed on the kitchen floor. By that time, we three aid men in the company, T/3 (Technician 3rd Class) Nagurney, Pfc. Lipson, and I, had decided we better each take a platoon and stay with it, for if all three of us stayed together there was always the chance of one shell getting us all and leaving the company without medical aid. So, I had been assigned to the first platoon, and it was in their house I slept that night.

Morning came to reveal that our battalion was all alone in that town of about fifty modern homes with no civilian anywhere in sight. In fact, we were told it was "open season" on all civilians and we were to shoot any we saw and ask questions later. Saarlautern, one of the largest cities on the Saar River and I believe the capital of the Saar district, was the town in which we had seen the shells exploding the night before. We were told that the 95th Infantry Division had originally taken the city several weeks before and had been lucky enough to secure a bridge intact. That evening we had to remove all identification from ourselves, our equipment, and our weapons and relieve the 95th Infantry Division (which was now in a holding position) without the enemy knowing it.

We were oriented on the situation in Saarlautern by members of the 95th Infantry Division, and they painted a picture for us that was hard to believe. The city was over three-fourths held by Americans and had at one time been all our territory. However, when the GI's had reached the extreme edge of town they found themselves facing the bulk of the Siegfried Line with rows of pillboxes lining the hills just outside of town. The suburbs of Saarlautern were composed of modern German homes and factories and so constructed that the basement of every house was a fortified pill-box with two feet of reinforced concrete walls and steel doors. In addition, every corner house was extra heavily fortified for strategic protection.

We were told that our principal duty in the city would be 24 hours guard duty to prevent a counter-attack from the Germans. We learned that we would have to be especially careful not to go out in the open in the daytime, for most of the streets were covered with machine gun, mortar, and artillery fire. We were also told that the enemy in that area respected the Red Cross brassard and would allow medics to go within ten yards or so of their positions to pick up wounded. That was a relief to me, for in Luxembourg we found that the Red Cross meant nothing to the enemy.

As dusk approached that evening we once again donned our equipment and started towards this strange city and a type of combat we had never before experienced. As we entered the outskirts of town we passed files of 95th Infantry Division men pulling bulky bed rolls loaded with quilts and other loot on sleds and wagons. They were in high spirits and said that for the most part they had enjoyed their stay in Saarlautern. I couldn't understand anyone's liking any part of the war, but I soon found out that Saarlautern wasn't half bad - that is in the reserve position we held at first.

Quietly picking our way through the rubble and wreckage of the still burning main industrial area of town, we soon reached the banks of the Saar River. Crossing it was a heavy stone bridge with sentries standing guard all along it in the holes the enemy artillery had dug-in an effort to destroy the structure. That was the only bridge across the river at that time, and our positions were the most eastward of any Allied positions. Ahead of us lay the densest part of the Siegfried Line with 35 miles of pill boxes, tank traps, and other emplacements. It had been a lucky break for our troops to take the bridge, but we lived in constant fear that someday the enemy might destroy it and leave us stranded at their mercy on the eastern banks of the Saar.

Turning right on the far side of the bridge and following up the river for a way, we came to the first group of houses and turned eastward. By that time, we were all overly anxious and careful lest we make the slightest noise, for we knew we must be very close to the enemy and remembered what we had been told about machine gun and mortar fire. After passing a few blocks of closely placed houses surrounded by knocked out German and American tanks, we finally halted in front of one building which appeared to be in better shape than the rest. This, we were told, would be the Company CP and that is where I was to be stationed so I could handle casualties from the first and weapons platoon. The second platoon became divorced from our company for our stay in Saarlautern and was attached to Love Company of our regiment's third battalion.

Upon entering the basement of the building, I was to stay in, I noticed a heavy steel door with sand bags placed in front of it to protect the entrance. Behind these bags a guard stood on duty 24 hours a day. Going on into the basement, I found, as I had been told, heavily reinforced walls and ceilings. After that no one could tell me Germany hadn't been planning this war for years. The basement was composed of a number of rooms with only one window in the entire basement. That very small window was in my room, but it had been heavily boarded and sandbagged to stop shell fragments. Each room had a small coal stove in it, and we found plenty of coal and coke in the neighborhood to keep us comfortably warm all the time. The only thing we lacked was some form of electric lights, for all the time we were there we had to burn candle wax from a near-by factory in "C" ration cans with a rag for a wick. Every hour or so we would have to chop off another piece of wax and refill the can.

When we first moved into our cellar I was told I could sleep in the runners' room, but I could see from the beginning that I was going to be bored to death with nothing to do all day. So, I volunteered to help Fairfield and Cunningham on the communications since that had been my job in combat before I joined the medics. Although most people don't realize it, in combat all messages use code names - especially over the radio or telephone lines; and since I was the only person in the company who was familiar with the codes and names besides Fairfield and Cunningham, they were more than glad to welcome me in the communications room with them. I was glad to be there, for besides giving me something to pass the time away with, it would give me the chance to live once again with my old friends. We had two "EE-8a" telephones (the kind with a crank on the side) and one sound-power phone (an instrument consisting of a handset only - for short distance communications only) to watch all the time and maintain the lines for them. The two large phones ran to the first and third battalion CP's, and the sound power was connected to a party line of seven phones to all of our platoons and outposts. Since this phone had no bell, we would have to whistle over it several times and then shout the code name of the party we wanted.

After two days at Saarlouis, the real name for the suburban part of Saarlautern we occupied, the snow began to thaw, and the river began to rise. In just a few hours the river had completely flooded the road we came in on and slowed down our supply lines. Before that time our kitchen, which was set up across the river, would send up two hot meals a day by jeep, and a "K" or "C" ration would keep us from starving in between meals. We had to keep an emergency supply of rations on hand in case the Krauts blew the bridge, and for the first two days of high water we had to live on those alone. Finally, the jeep drivers found another road to us that wasn't mined or underwater so once again we had hot meals.

I remember a favorite concoction we used to have every day in both Saarlautern and Luxembourg before the snow melted. We would take a little condensed milk from a Ten-in-One Ration and mix it with sugar and lemon or orange powder from "K" or "C" rations to form a paste. Then we would fill the canteen cup with fresh snow and stir it in until we had a delicious sherbet. We could also make delicious chocolate sherbet without milk by using cocoa and water with snow.

At first Fairfield, Cunningham, and I would divide the night up into three four-hour shifts and rotate these every night. I didn't mind the four-hour period, for it was quiet and provided a swell time for me to write letters and read magazines. I wrote that long letter you had printed in the Webster News-Times one night while I was watching the telephone in that basement in Saarlouis. Every hour on the hour we would have to check in to battalion and report anything unusual that had been reported in to us by the platoons on their half-hour reports. The only bad part I found about living in that basement was that the greasy smoke of the candles burning 24 hours a day was irritating our throats and coating our clothing with soot. However, the safety it provided for us more than made up for any of its shortcomings.

After a few days of four-hour night shifts we had S/Sgt. George Samsel, one of the company runners, move in with us. Since we only had three beds it was a race to bed every night to see who would start out on the best bed. We had to play "hot bed" throughout the night - that is the man coming off duty would have to take the bed of the man relieving him.

Samsel was really a welcome addition to our communications group, for he was the intellectual type with a very refreshing and original sense of humor. He had a little Louisiana belle for a wife, even though he was a Philadelphia Yankee. Although his parents were well to do and provided him with everything he needed in life (he used to boast he had never worked a day in his life), he was anything but spoiled. After a few days together, George and I became the best of friends, and he used to kid me about fixing him up if he ever got hit.

The first morning after we arrived in Saarlautern, my curiosity got the best of me, and I decided I had to explore the rest of the house. The only accessible entrance was the back door, and I had to climb over piles of rubble to get to it. Inside, I found empty "K" ration boxes and other refuse that relieved my fears about any booby traps. I knew that other GI's had lived there before. The men we relieved said they had received orders that since they were now in Germany they were to wreck everything; and believe me, they really did. All the furniture had been either destroyed by shells or our own men, and they had even gone so far as to defecate in every corner and drawer of every room. They explained this by saying that it was never safe at first to go outside for anything, so they were forced to relieve themselves inside. I found a foot pedal organ in the living room to be the only article that hadn't been damaged; and since I have always had a secret ambition to play one, I finally had my chance to realize this desire in that partially destroyed home in Saarlouis.

Proceeding on with my tour, I discovered the very modern house had three stories plus an attic, but the top two had been badly damaged by shell fire. I discovered several Nazi and German flags on the third floor and sent two of them home in one of my letters. The attic contained several large rooms in it plus a darkroom, which had been completely ransacked. Several hundred feet of movie film lined the floor and trailed down the stairs and throughout the house.

Using old radio batteries for power, I was able to rig up an electric light for our basement room. After the first day we found that even a new battery only lasted about 24 hours, so we had to resort to the candles except on special occasions.

In the following diagram I have roughly represented the layout of our company and the houses it occupied. We were several hundred yards from the front lines in a reserve position but received a great deal of enemy artillery and mortar fire. Directly behind the house we occupied was a completely destroyed pill box with walls of from ten to twelve feet of reinforced concrete. It was cleverly camouflaged before our troops captured and destroyed it and must have looked exactly like a small house. There were windows painted on its walls and a pyramidal wooden roof built over it. There was a fence and garden around it, so I imagine our troops were completely surprised to find it to be a heavily fortified pill box. We were told it required 1,800 pounds of demolitions to blow it up, so you can imagine how well constructed it was.

As I mentioned before, we were safe as long as we stayed within the confines of our basement prison, but it was necessary to venture out to the back yards several times a day to get to the slit trench latrine we had constructed. I remember two different times I was caught there literally with my pants down when enemy long-range machine gun fire started chipping the brick wall away right over my head. It was a very embarrassing situation to say the least, and one in which I had to decide whether I would rather sacrifice myself or my pride and dignity.

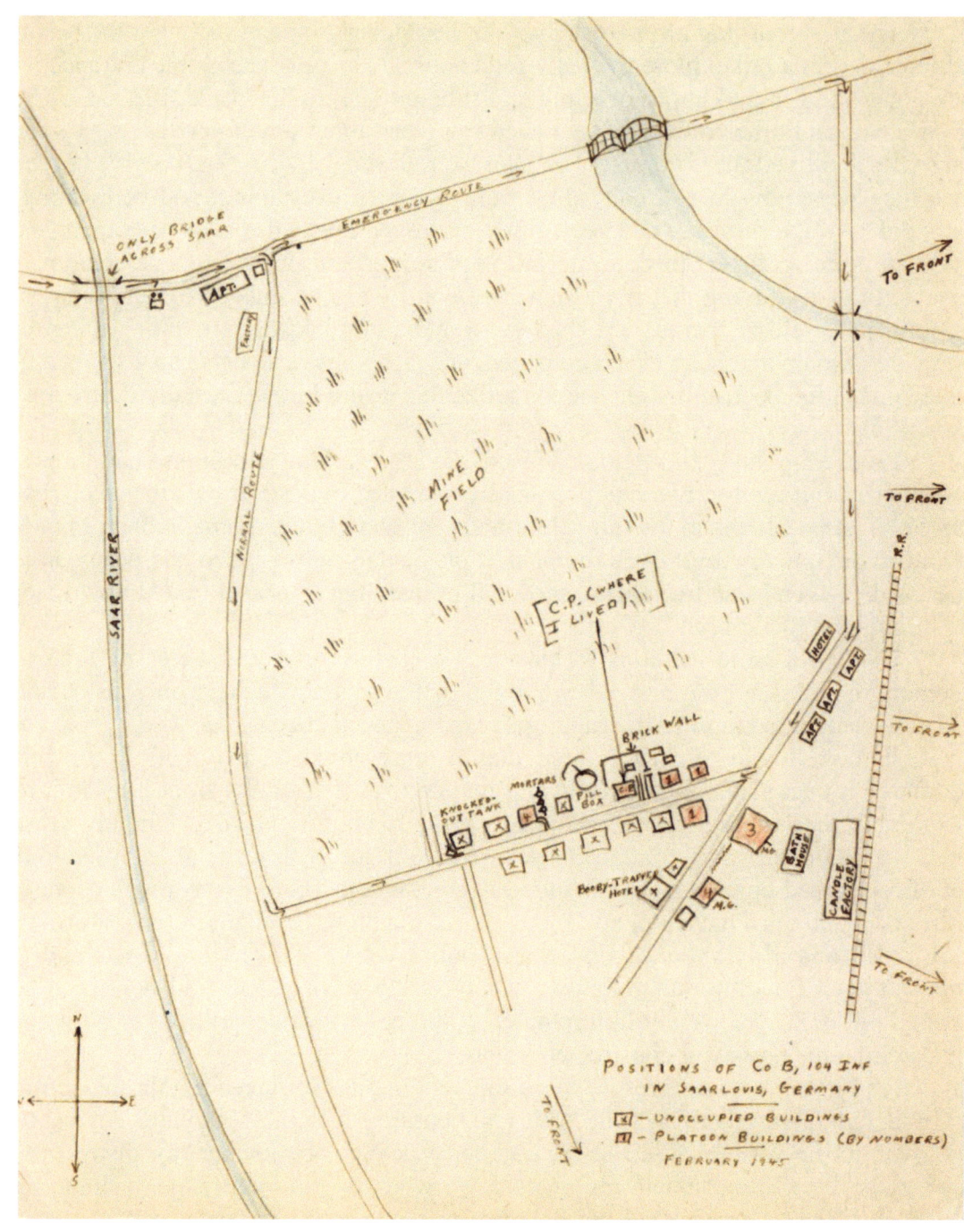

Hand-drawn map of home in Saarlouis, showing nearby minefield, candle factory, and hidden pillbox

James's hand-drawn map of the street in Saarlouis where he lived in the basement of the indicated house. Gary visited the house in 2016 and interviewed the neighbor, who was 12 years old at the time and distinctly remembered the American GIs. The pillbox and the bullet holes in the brick wall in the back of the house are still plainly visible. Map by James Cutter; caption by Gary Cutter

Discovery of hidden pillbox in Saarlouis

James's historic map revealed the otherwise unknown pillbox in the backyard where he stayed during the war. Local historians were thrilled to find it after viewing the map, as it had been hidden and shrouded in shrubbery for decades.
Photo by Gary Cutter; caption by Gary Cutter

Discovery of bullet-scarred brick wall behind Saarlouis house

The brick wall in the backyard of the house indicated on James's hand-drawn map was mostly covered in ivy during my 2016 visit. However, pulling the ivy aside revealed a line of bullet holes—exactly as described in his book.
Photo by Gary Cutter; caption by Gary Cutter

We had been warned before we entered the town that it was lousy with mines and booby traps - both our own and German. All of the roads were lined with mines and most of the houses that weren't occupied contained both German and American mines. In fact, the hotel our third platoon occupied had several of the rooms booby-trapped, and the men had to constantly remind themselves not to try any closed doors. Two months after the war was over I read and sent you an article in the Stars and Stripes (US Army Newspaper) stating that an average of ten people a day are still being killed. I imagine people will still be getting killed from mines for several years after V-E Day, for most of them are cleverly concealed.

After a few days in the basement I decided I would explore some of the nearby houses that were supposed to be safe. The object of my searching was to find things that would make living more comfortable for us: for example, mattresses, eating utensils, stationery, and canned fruit. I found a great deal of the latter in the form of preserved cherries, pears, peaches, and apple sauce, but the omission of sugar from them, caused by the shortage in Germany, made most of them unpalatable. However, I did find some things which would help pass the time away. Altogether I rounded up about a dozen German telephones and a half dozen radios. One phone, which we found in an old brewery, was really a miniature switchboard, so I rigged up an inter-office phone between our communications room and the CO's room. He was always receiving calls from Battalion and the platoons, so I fixed up the switch board affair so by merely flipping a switch we could connect him with either of the two outside lines. I found several old door bells and batteries; so, I fixed them up in such a manner that, by turning the dial on our phone, it would ring a buzzer in Captain Stout's room. And by turning his dial, he could ring us. I had a great deal of fun in my spare time with those German phones and was able to tie in more platoons via telephone by employing them.

From a medical standpoint Saarlouis was not a very good set-up. Our battalion aid station was inaccessible in daytime because of open stretches with enemy observation, and the only way we could get men to the doctor in daylight was via jeep, which was usually crowded. Jeep travel was dangerous, too, for few jeeps ever passed without being followed right down the road with mortar shells. So, the only way to handle sick call was for me to go out to see all of the men and order any medicine over the telephone. Quite a few of the men developed diarrhea from eating so many French-fried potatoes (we lived on them between meals), so I had to keep a bottle of Camphorated Opium on hand all the time for that. Also, most of the men had bad coughs from the candle smoke, so I furnished them with cough syrup and troches. I still think some of those fellows were taking that cough syrup because of its alcohol content, but I could never prove it!

We had an exciting experience the third night we were in Saarlouis. Most of the fellows were still a little jittery because of the newness of the situation. On top of that, it was such a dark night that even the parachute illumination flares our mortars sent up would not penetrate the fog. I was on duty from 0200 to 0600 on that night when thaws were just beginning. I was getting rather drowsy when I heard a quiet but excited whistle on the sound-power telephone. I answered it and heard someone rattle off something in such an excited manner I couldn't understand it. Finally, after several repetitions I made out that he was trying to tell me that there was someone out in back of his house - two doors up from where I was. The guard had challenged the person, and the noises had stopped for a while. Then the person continued walking.

He had just finished talking to me when I heard the explosion of a hand grenade out in back quickly followed by another. Then came nothing but minutes of silence. I whistled in vain for him over the phone. Finally, I decided I had better see what was up, so I took Fairfield's .45 and went outside to where our guards stood. They had no idea what was going on, but when I told them about the other fellow hearing the footsteps they confirmed his story by saying they had heard them also. I went back inside and found the first fellow whistling for me. He said he didn't know what it was, but whatever it had been had stopped making noises now.

I called our mortars and asked for three or four flares, but their brilliance still couldn't penetrate the fog. At that minute I heard three more hand grenades go off right in our back yard, and another voice started calling over the phone. This time it was the mortar section saying they had heard footsteps too but hadn't thrown any grenades. I checked with my own guards and found they had thrown the last three grenades at the "footsteps." Then everything had become quiet, so they started boasting about how they "got him!" A little while later the weapons platoon threw a couple of grenades, so everyone was happy that the footsteps were quiet.

The next morning, we went out to pick up the bodies of our victims and found that the "footsteps" had been nothing else but the ice cracking and dropping from the trees in the back yards!

We were really beginning to enjoy our stay in Saarlautern and wishing we could stay there for the rest of the war when Captain Stout received orders to move out another platoon to go up on line and help out Love Company. Needless to say, he picked the first platoon, so we rolled up our packs and said our last farewells to our friends we were leaving behind. As you know, our second platoon had been with Love Company all the time, and one of their men was killed the first night we were there by mortar fragments coming in the open window where he was standing guard. That didn't help our feelings about going up there at all, for even if a mortar didn't get us, we felt sure a mine would.

I'll never forget that walk up to our new positions. Lt. Schmutz (our platoon leader), and Captain Stout decided they would go out and reconnoiter the route, for they felt sure it would be a snap. They had forgotten that some of our troops were making an attack that night and the Krauts had one of the streets we were to use completely covered with grazing machine gun fire. It was too low to crawl under and too continuous to try to run in between bursts. They told us tracers were bouncing off the streets like rain, so we waited until around midnight before starting. By that time things were pretty well quiet except for an occasional shell or two. We cautiously tip-toed up the street, past an apartment house, through an old warehouse littered with pots and pans (which clattered every time someone stepped on them), down the street, under a railroad viaduct, and up the street to the Love Company CP We were relieved to have reached our destination safely as a group and were ready to settle down when Lt. Schmutz returned from the CP with the news that we were to go right up on line to one of the furthermost outposts.

So, we once more prepared ourselves for a nerve-wracking trip, but it turned out to be ten times worse than we expected. Chase, one of the fellows who had slept in the foxhole next to mine up in Kaundorf (and the only one of three men left), was to serve as our guide to the outpost. Chase is a very nervy sort of guy who seldom ever recognizes danger or fear, so when he told us it was a rough and dangerous trip up there we knew he really meant it! Our platoon was split up into three groups, so I went with the most forward outpost where the casualties would probably be the heaviest.

We left the Love Company CP and slowly picked our way up the street through all the bricks and rubbish of the almost completely destroyed houses on either side. The most that was left of any of them was a burned-out shell, and we were forced to duck low between them to avoid the stray bullets that sprayed through the empty spaces. Reaching the corner, we faced a long open field on the other side of which was a small river with a foot bridge crossing it. The bridge seemed to be a perfect target for the enemy, and Chase warned us to keep quiet and "run like hell," for the enemy had direct observation with machine gun fire on the span.

Well, run we did, and a few seconds after we were all across we saw what he meant. A stream of tracers poured into the little plank bridge from a stationary gun the Heinies had zeroed-in on it all the time. From the bridge to the next row of buildings was about 50 yards of open field again, so we completed the dash across as rapidly as possible, dodging fence posts and wire along the way.

Half-way up the next block we turned and went through the hall of a battered-up apartment house and out through the back yard. Keeping close to the backs of those houses, we followed up beside another small stream, being careful not to step off the path for fear of the mines which lined it. We turned into the next street and were halted by Case at the corner. "Over there is where we are going, but I'm going on ahead to tip off the guard you are coming so he won't shoot you. Stay here until I get back," he warned. I'm thankful now that he did go ahead, for the guards had orders to shoot and then ask questions, and had we been challenged in the middle of the street we would have been caught in the grazing fire which intermittently streamed down the street.

When we were all safe in the basement of our new home, we were once more oriented by the former occupants. They warned us that all of the houses in that vicinity had been mined several times by both sides. All of the buildings had changed hands at least three different times, and each occupant added his own booby traps to the already accumulated collection. In other words, we could expect every house to be completely booby-trapped from the basement to the roof.

The next morning, we found there were no rations for us, and the only time they could be brought up was after dark. We hollered, pleaded, and even offered to go after them ourselves if they would only give them to us, but it wasn't until late that night we received any. By that time, I has so hungry I would have eaten anything, and a borrowed can of pork and egg yolks tasted mighty good! Lt. Schmutz heated them up in a skillet over a small squad stove we borrowed, and then three of us sat down and gobbled them up as fast as we could, eating them out of the frying pan, our only utensil.

After we had all finished we were sitting there quietly when Lt. Schmutz broke out laughing. In reply to our questions he laughed again and replied, "I was just thinking how silly some of this army life seems - how different it is from the trivial stuff in the States. Take this for example. Here we are, the three of us eating out of the same pan, and back in the States they won't even let officers and enlisted men associate with each other or even eat in the same mess hall with each other. Isn't that the silliest damn thing you've ever heard of?" And right there he summed up in a few sentences what made him such a good officer and such an excellent leader. In combat he knows no rank differences. He only knows he has a job to do and a bunch of buddies along with him to help him do it. He always had the complete backing of his men, and as long as he remains as he now is he will continue to have that support.

The following day, one of the platoons of Love Company jumped off in the attack to finish clearing out the Krauts in our block. The way we had been living, the enemy was housed in the building in our back yard that faced out on the next street over. The two houses weren't over 25 yards apart, and our neighbors weren't the agreeable type such as you find in most city blocks. So, we were somewhat relieved when friendly troops moved in and the Heinies moved out that day. However, in the process many of our men were wounded by mortar fire, grenades, and mines, and since I was the closest aid man I had to patch most of them up. One or two of the men had their feet removed by the small German shoe mines, and still others had their faces and hands torn to shreds by "S" (Bouncing Betsy) mines. Those booby traps are wicked things and usually permanently disfigure or cripple a man.

After three days with Love Company we returned to our own outfit - back to what we had learned to call home! The next day we pulled back to Falch, France, another holding position with the enemy across the river from us. The river was several miles from us, so we were far from any battle and considered the place a rest area. Battalion headquarters must have felt the same way about it, for they started a program of close order drills, calisthenics, and road marches. While in Falch, I was delighted to have Bill Jaffe, my old friend from the Nieu Amsterdam and 17th Replacement Depot drop in on me for a visit. I discovered he was in the same division with me and was attached to the division CIC (counter-intelligence corps). Of course, he was strictly non-combatant and had a racket if I have ever seen one. It was a treat to see him again, though, for he had heard from some of the old friends who came over with us; and he is an interesting conversationalist.

Our rest period was interrupted when we were suddenly called back to Saarlautern and back to our old buildings. When I returned that time I really made use of the opportunity to loot everything possible. I went into all of the houses for blocks around and really had a dandy time with all the stuff I collected. Tex set up a regular workshop in the house he had, complete with everything from a drill press to a forge and anvil. He used to take files and make beautiful knives out of them with decorative brass handles and old cartridges for the hilt and handles.

The enemy had been hitting close to our positions all of the time and had scored one or two direct hits on the top of the five-story hotel our third platoon was in: they must have found out, somehow, that we were using the upstairs for an artillery observers outpost. One day they started working the top floors over, and before they had finished there has little left of the fourth, fifth, and attic floors. Luckily no one was up there at the time.

After three days back at Saarlautern, our battalion finally received the week in reserve we had been promised. We were withdrawn to the town of Uberherrn on February 19 and remained there until the 27th During our stay there we enjoyed nothing but peace and quiet, and, of course, chicken. "Chicken" is the army name for the little nerve-wracking details of basic training and army garrison life. Such things as having your jackets fully buttoned at all times, shining your shoes, having inspections, and taking training during a rest period are considered "chicken" to the GI's. There was beaucoup (French for large quantity) chicken at Uberherrn; but it was wonderful to have it thrown at you instead of shells and bullets, and we loved it for a change. It really felt good to shave every day, keep our clothes clean, and watch how we dressed. We did it all out of personal pride anyway, and no order was necessary for most of us.

On the 25th of February, I received one of the most pleasant surprises of my army life. I got a pass to Metz, where the YD had set up what I had heard was a wonderful rest camp called "The Yankee Hotel.".

CHAPTER VI

After a long, dusty truck ride from Uberherrn to Metz, France, our rest camp group stopped in front of a luxurious looking, ultra-modern building renamed the "Yankee Hotel." We were led inside the four-story structure by an ex-combat man, who had been wounded and given a limited assignment. We were told that we had the run of the place and would be issued a pass good for the four days there in Metz. The only requirement was that we get off the streets by 2200 every evening. There were no formations; and we could sleep all four days we were there or could stay out on pass all day.

The first thing that interested me was the hot shower and clean clothes they offered. Next, I went down to the recreation room and tried out my game of Ping-Pong. Finding myself rather badly out of practice, I wandered over to the mess hall for chow. The meals were a treat and a rest in themselves. The food was delicious and served by really chic French waitresses!

Two of the men who accompanied me from the company were Dobrinski (my old friend from the machine gun section) and Maynard, a fairly new replacement whose parents were both Canadian. He spoke good French and proved invaluable as a translator. After dinner we walked around town for a while and saw some of the beautiful cathedrals and other sights of Metz. Most of the historic structures were damaged by the war - especially the bridges. One of the larger churches we went into made me sick to see the damage the war had dealt it. From the remains I could see that it had once been an exquisitely beautiful structure, but at that time the floors were littered with pieces of the ancient walls and roofs. The beautiful stained-glass windows had been shattered in many places, but the gold pulpit and large crucifix remained undamaged.

The Moselle River was jammed with the wreckage of many scuttled barges and destroyed bridges left behind by the retreating Germans. Many of them had been replaced by the unsightly, but serviceable, Bailey bridges of the US Corps of Engineers. Some of the old castles and forts were still standing in their pre-war ruins, but several of them had aged considerably during the current war.

Metz had changed a good deal since my stay there in December, but most of the shops had to remain closed because of the shortage of articles for sale. However, an American Red Cross Club named the "Gateway to Hell Club" was operating in one of the more fashionable downtown restaurants, and American soldiers were welcome to come in and buy as many doughnuts and cups of coffee as they desired. There were also several GI theaters operating throughout the day for the entertainment of men on pass.

Before going to Metz, I had received a letter from Dick (Thompson, my sister Buff's husband) saying he was in France not too far from me. He described his hospital as

39

being set up in an old college, so right off the bat I guessed he was in Nancy. Of course, he could have been in any of a dozen large French towns and still answer that brief description, but after that second day in Metz I visited an Army Post Office and inquired where the 173rd General Hospital was set up at the time. With some reluctance and arguing that he wasn't allowed to give that information out, the clerk finally pulled out his lists and told me it was still in Nancy. I was glad to know where he was but still didn't seriously consider visiting him, for Nancy is about 35 miles from Metz. Besides, the clerk at the Yankee Hotel told me he couldn't give me a pass outside of Metz and I would be AWOL if I went any other way. I asked him how the MP's were around there and if they were very nosy. He just winked and said he didn't know.

That evening I was talking to Maynard when he mentioned that he had a girlfriend in Nancy and would certainly like to visit her. That settled things right then and there. If two of us went along together it would be much safer, so the next morning found us out on the main highway to Nancy with our thumbs in the air.

A colored quartermaster driver picked us up after about a half hour and took us right into Nancy. He didn't know where the 173rd General Hospital was, but he said he would let me off at the one he was most familiar with. He dropped me off there, but it turned out to be about four miles from Dick's unit.

As soon as I was on the streets I noticed my mistake. Metz was in a combat zone where steel helmets, cartridge belts, and weapons (or Red Cross brassards) were worn; but Nancy was strictly non-combatant with everyone wearing garrison caps and no belts or brassards. I knew I stuck out like a sore thumb in the crowd, but luckily no MP stopped me and asked me for my pass. Next, I noticed that Nancy was nothing like Metz. It was hardly damaged, all the shops were open for business with large stocks, and the trolleys were running just like peace time. After wandering on the main street for an hour I finally found a medic who knew where the 173rd General Hospital was. Every one of the dozen other hospitals in town was clearly marked on every street corner with a large Red Cross and direction arrow, but the 173rd General Hospital had refrained from their use. I was almost beginning to believe that the hospital had suddenly pulled out of the city a few days before. Finally, I rounded a corner to be greeted by a large sign with the words "173rd General Hospital" wiping the despair out of my mind. The hospital covered several full blocks of ground with a large group of buildings in the center. Surrounding the plot was a high wire fence with armed guards stationed at the only entrance.

Passing quickly by the sentries with a smile and a nod (which must have taken them by surprise), I proceeded directly to the administration building. Realizing how large the personnel force must be for such a large hospital, I decided my only hope of finding Dick was to inquire for him at message center. Later I discovered that I might have stopped anyone and asked for "Thompson," for he apparently was known by one and all - from the brass to the lowest buck private. Inside the building I discovered things to be almost deserted, but in the message center was one staff sergeant still on duty. He immediately informed me that Dick was probably in the chow line and indicated the location of the building.

Slowly ambling over to the mess hall on my then painful feet, I began to wonder if I would have to walk the entire length of the line and inspect every face before finding the countenance that would flash familiarity in my mind. That was hardly necessary, for as soon as I neared the line I heard someone call out, "who are you looking for, stranger?"

and was aware of Dick running towards me with his mess kit in one hand and his other hand waving in the air. I can't possibly explain how relieved and wonderful I felt just to see him again, and I realized that all of the chances I had taken to get there were worthwhile just for that one moment.

Dick hadn't changed as much as I thought I had. He was the same old "happy go lucky" Dick and just as sincere as ever. True, it was the first time I had seen him in that disgrace to clothing the army calls fatigues, and the faded green hat with the round brim pushed well back seemed unnatural on his usually bare head. But Dick was the same. He quickly grabbed my arm and led me back to his place in line, where I shook hands with at least a dozen different men and tried to remember 12 different names and faces.

Then he realized that it was time to eat and rushed me up to his barracks room. There I met George, one of his best friends, who slept underneath him in the doubled-decked bed. At the present time George is the only name I can recall from the hundreds I was introduced to that day. While borrowing a mess kit for me, Dick presented me to several more friends who were busily engaged in bunk fatigue (sleeping). Then I was rushed back to the chow line carrying a borrowed mess kit and wearing a borrowed cap in place of my helmet liner. Come to think of it, that was the first time I had anything on my head besides a helmet for five months, and that is the only time I wore a garrison cap for more than nine months.

Wielding his usual influence, Dick was able to persuade the cooks into feeding me with the rest of the regular hospital personnel, and after the long morning I had just put in even the dehydrated hash tasted good. Of course, during the entire dinner meal I was introduced to many more of Dick's friends, whose names I promptly forgot.

Luckily Dick was able to get off duty that afternoon and evening, and even though a special meeting was called that afternoon and all passes canceled, Dick, with his usual persuasive powers was able to talk the first sergeant and a lieutenant out of a pass

That afternoon was another real adventure that I will be long in forgetting. The one thing I really wanted to do was to have a portrait made for Mother's birthday, so we completed that detail on the first lap of our tour of Nancy. (The small cap I am wearing was borrowed from Dick. The Combat Infantryman's Badge, awarded only in combat, was regarded with awe in rear areas.)

The next few hours passed swiftly in an aimless wandering through the main streets, shops, and market places of the colorful city. I could hardly believe that such a place still existed with all shops open for business and none of the buildings wrecked. I was able to pick up a few souvenirs, which Dick later sent home in a combined package from the two of us. I was also treated to the unfamiliar sound of American music at one or two of the restaurants; and although it didn't sound exactly like Tommy Dorsey or Glenn Miller, the French musicians did an amiable job at the task of interpreting American swing music.

The afternoon passed all too rapidly, and before I knew it, it was late in the evening and time to retire; for Dick still had a full day's work ahead of him the next day. Luckily, George wasn't going to use his bed that night, for he was assigned to night duty.

Before turning in we both felt an intense hunger, for while wandering around town we had failed to return in time for supper. Again, Dick came to the rescue and called upon his friends in the kitchen. Sticking his head through a small opening in the door, he appealed to one of the cook's sympathy. His efforts were soon repaid with a hand-full of sizzling pork chops and a stack of bread. To us it seemed like a feast, and we quickly devoured the food in the seclusion of an unused building.

Portrait taken in Nancy, France for Mother's birthday

James had this portrait made in Nancy, France while technically AWOL, as a birthday gift for his mother. He arrived wearing only his combat helmet—an unmistakable sign he wasn't authorized to be there—so he borrowed a cap a size too small from his brother-in-law Dick.
Photo by studio photographer; caption by Gary Cutter

Not knowing how long it would take me to return to Metz, I left Dick the next morning immediately after breakfast. I'll never forget the emptiness I felt inside myself and the huge lump that developed in my throat. It was a foggy morning, and Dick followed me across the open field directly in front of the hospital. I don't remember what I said or did then, for the thick and silent fog seemed to swallow up everything in the darkness of the morning. I just remember that I wanted to leave quickly before I revealed what a struggle I was having within myself, and before I showed what a horror the thought of returning to combat held for me. We shook hands, and the next thing I remember is walking down the main road to Metz with my thumb in the air. A sympathetic French soldier in his converted GI truck finally picked me up and gave me the first of the seven rides it required to return to the Yankee hotel.

Arriving at Metz in time for dinner, I found it hard to believe I had returned to the same city I had been in just the preceding day. The city had lost all of its appeal, for Nancy had spoiled me. I had tasted 12 hours of the freedom of a part of the world not engaged in combat and unaffected by the swift passage through of American troops on their mad dash across France the previous Fall

The pass to Metz ended entirely too soon, and before I realized what was happening I was on a truck going back to the company. I had learned from the men just arriving at the rest camp that our battalion had moved from its position of rest and was once again engaged in combat. I felt a new fear as I drew closer to our positions; and then I realized what the wounded men being returned back to the companies from the hospitals had meant when they said, "It's ten times as hard to go into combat the second time as it was the first." When I returned from the clearing company the other two times, I discovered in part what they meant; but after tasting the outside world again, I found that it was a terrific mental feat to force myself back up there on the line. As soon as I reached the battalion CP in Oberesch, Germany, I once again became resigned to my fate and felt the tension and nervous expectation of combat return.

CHAPTER VII

Baker Company, from February 27 until March 5, was split up into three different towns with two platoons out posting in two small towns on the river. Before I had left the battalion for rest camp, the regimental detachment first sergeant had casually mentioned to me that my rating as a buck sergeant did not fit into the TO (table of organization) and that I would have to be busted (demoted). He quickly assured me, though, that the first opening that came along I would be returned to my same pay with the rating of T/4; but I knew that was just a consoling statement made in an effort to pacify me. I immediately reacted to his announcement as a man who has just received a blow from the rear. When I joined the medics, I was assured that I would always retain my rating. If it did change, I would receive a promotion rather than a demotion. During the two months I was an aid man I found out that the medic's job is much more dangerous than that of the average infantry man, so it occurred to me that I was being double crossed.

Before I left for Metz I applied for a transfer back to the infantry, for Captain Stout had promised me my old job back and more than welcomed me. The words he spoke the day I told him about being transferred out of the company up in Luxembourg still rang in my ears, "Damn, the best damn man in the company!" I know he had over rated me considerably, but I knew I still had a home if I desired to return to the company as an infantry man. While I was in Oberesch I stopped by the aid station to find out whether I should pick up my old aid kits or draw a carbine. They informed me that the transfer hadn't come through yet, so I returned to the Company with my aid kits.

Baker Company CP and first platoon were located in a small town named Guerlfangen with the second platoon in Emersdorf and the third platoon in Femersdorf. Both of the two out posting towns were located right on the river, and directly across the water was the enemy. The lines had remained that way for several weeks, and our orders were simply to hold the ground. From the maps we had we were able to judge that we were approximately 12 to 15 miles due north of Saarlautern with part of the division still occupying that city. Guerlfangen is three or four miles away from both of the outpost villages, and the only means of communications was via narrow, muddy roads.

Suspecting my transfer would come through any day, I told Captain Stout I would gladly do both my proposed infantry job and medical duties until the official transfer arrived. Again, I slept in the CP communications room with Fairfield and Cunningham. A part of the morning would be devoted to visiting the men of my platoon to see if any of them had taken sick, and the rest of the day was devoted to maintenance of the communication lines.

The situation in both of the outpost towns was a queer one, for from nearly every house it was possible to detect enemy personnel walking around on the streets of the large town directly across the river. If we fired nothing at the enemy, they would fire nothing at us. One day our mortar platoon became ambitious enough to fire six rounds into the enemy held town. Several hours later they received exactly six German shells in their town. From then on, we decided it was a game of an eye for an eye, and since our job was purely one of holding ground, we didn't attempt the offensive any more.

However, one day Lt. Colonel Gladding (our battalion commander, a swaggering National Guardsman whose civilian occupation was delivering blocks of ice to customers) decided the enemy targets were too good to pass up, so he ordered some tanks to proceed to the high hill above the river and shoot any visible pill boxes. That was a great mistake, for as soon as our tanks had fired and withdrawn all hell broke loose; and from then on it wasn't safe to enter either town in daylight. As a result of the ten minutes fun the tankers had firing across the river, our company suffered one man killed and several wounded. Besides that, it made our job of tracing communications wires much more dangerous. The wires were more frequently knocked out, too, for the Krauts sprinkled scattered shells into our positions all day long.

The company CP, where our communications center was installed, was located in the priest house of the town, the least damaged of the hopelessly ruined homes. In our room we had six different telephones and if ever a switchboard was needed it was in that position. I again installed the CO's private phone in his office for him, so he could answer any incoming calls without leaving his room. With six different telephone lines to maintain throughout the many barrages you can easily see that most of our time - both day and night - was spent repairing breaks. Often, we would go to bed at night with all lines working perfectly and wake up the next morning to find half of them dead. We couldn't allow any telephone to be out of commission for more than a few hours, for an enemy attack was anticipated at any time. If it did come at one of our platoon outposts, they would have to inform us and then withdraw to a safer defensive position. Since our only means of speedy communication was via telephone, we had to keep on our toes all of the time to detect and repair breaks immediately.

I can still remember several dark, rainy nights of trying to trace a three-mile wire to discover breaks. To make things more interesting, the wires passed through several known mine fields; and in the night the markers were indiscernible. The only way to trace a wire at night is to pick it up in your bare hands and feel for breaks or short circuits. A favorite trick of the enemy (and we were conscious of enemy patrols working behind our lines), was to cut the wires and then set up an ambush for wiremen coming to repair the break. Add to all of these hazards the icy coldness of a February rain in Germany, and you have a very undesirable predicament; but nevertheless, a situation much safer than a medic finds himself in combat. As long as I remained with the CP I was at least sure of sleeping in a house if anyone in the company did, for the CP always chose the best house in every town.

Another feature that interested me in Guerlfangen was the large church directly across from our priest house. Aside from a few small shell holes in the roof, the church was undamaged. I decided to explore it. Being cautious of mines, I careful tiptoed down the main aisle of the Catholic church and up to the beautifully gilded alter. For such a small town the church was amazingly beautiful and elaborate inside. After a brief look inside, I discovered what I wanted right away, for up in the choir loft sat a large pipe organ. As long as I have wanted to, I had never had the opportunity to play a two-manual pipe organ. Quickly examining the instrument, I realized it was completely undamaged; but the electricity in the town had been knocked out, so I decided it was hopeless to try to use it. Before leaving the edifice, I climbed up the steep circular stairs in the anteroom towards the bell tower. When I reached the first landing I discovered I was directly behind the organ, and right beside me were the huge bellows, on one end of which was a badly worn foot pedal. A deep pit was worn in the stone floor on each side of the pedal where for many years the organ boys had stood on one foot at a time while pumping with the other.

Church in Guerlfangen, 2016

During the war, my father explored this church across from the "priest house" where he was quartered. Though the roof had suffered minor shell damage, the ornate interior and two-manual pipe organ remained intact. With help from a reluctant "organ boy," he managed to play the instrument briefly—fulfilling a lifelong dream. Photo by Gary Cutter; caption by Gary Cutter

All I had to do then was talk some husky fellow into being organ boy for me, so I chose one of the CP guards named Blakely, a fellow with a great deal more brawn than brains. He pumped with all his might for about five minutes and then quit. I tried to explain to him that he was wasting half his effort, for once the bellows was full it wasn't necessary to add more air until a pointer had gone down past a certain point. His stamina had played out, though, and he refused to pump even one more time for me. Oh, well, I can still say I have played a pipe organ even though it was only for five minutes.

There was a fellow in the first platoon, though, who could really play a piano. His name was Lucky Newman, and he had more luck at finding organ boys than I did. In fact, the fellows in the platoon used to volunteer to pump the organ for him just to hear him play. Later on, I found a small foot pedal organ in the house next to ours, so we wheeled it up to his quarters, so he could entertain us with concerts - mainly composed of swing.

The pipe organ James played in Guerlfangen, 1945

In March 2016, I visited Guerlfangen and found the church still standing. Though remodeled, the pipe organ my father had briefly played during the war remained original. With help from local historian Fred Fey, I arranged the visit in advance and was warmly welcomed. A town dignitary presented me with a book of local history, and the church organist played for my wife and me—on the organ my father had once played over 70 years before.
Photo by Gary Cutter; caption by Gary Cutter

Once or twice a week the civilians, who had been evacuated from the town, were allowed to return to obtain food for their livestock. One day I was walking through the ruins of what had once been a house, when the civilian owner arrived. It was the first time he had seen his house since the war had struck it. As he came through the remains of the door, the aged man fell forward on his knees and began crying like a woman. He sifted the sand and chipped bricks that lay on the floor through his hands and sobbed louder. Looking around at the rest of the burned-out rooms, he buried his head still deeper in his hands and gasped for breath. I stood there and watched his performance for several minutes, and at first, I felt sorry for him. Then I looked around the room and saw a large portrait of Hitler adorning the wall with a hole in it where some GI had run his bayonet through. Still remaining in the refuse were several other articles confirming his association with the Nazi party. I no longer felt sorry for him, but instead I wanted to go over where he crouched and give him a good swift kick on his protruding posterior.

After a little while he looked to me for sympathy, and I felt like pointing my carbine at him and scaring him half to death. His kind started the war, his kind fought the war, and his kind killed those dead buddies of mine just as sure as the German in uniform who aimed the gun. He had been fearless and domineering while his side was winning, and he had supported the Nazis with everything he had they could use. Now his side was losing; and he looked to me for sympathy, when he should have been carrying a rifle like the rest of the enemy. I used what little German I knew to let him understand what I thought of him and then waved him back to his feed gathering with a carbine.

Even though we suffered casualties at Guerlfangen, the position could be considered one of rest compared to our previous days of combat. We knew it was too good to last and weren't surprised to learn that a new division, fresh from the States, was to relieve us. That division was the 65th Infantry Division.

0200, March 6, found us loading onto trucks in the confusion of the early morning darkness and rain. We weren't sure just where we were headed, but we all felt sure it was bound to lead to combat again. Our luck had held out too long. We had been in holding positions too long. It was quite a surprise, then, for us to find ourselves unloaded at the entrance of a modernistic German hospital in Irsch (near Saarburg) at noon that day. The kitchens set up and served hot meals to us as we straightened up the rooms for occupancy. Each platoon was given a small room, and some men were lucky enough to find small mattresses for sleeping on. For myself, though, I was satisfied to just curl up on the floor and sleep the day away, for I had been up all night helping to orient the green replacements from the 65th Infantry Division. I was just looking forward to a good night's sleep when we were ordered to move out. We had time for a quick supper and nothing else.

By the time we arrived at our destination via some colored boys' quartermaster trucks, we were fairly well puzzled. The trucks had driven all the way with their "cat's eyes" (small blackout headlights) on, a practice that is never used anywhere except at the front. Upon de-trucking we expected to have to hike several more miles to get into position for combat. But to our surprise, we walked a few hundred yards and stopped in a position where some 240 howitzers had been set up the day before and pulled out just before our arrival. Then the explanation came. The enemy was pulling a heavy counter-attack and we were placed in a position to stop them if they did get through.

The rest of the men started digging in while Fairfield and I crawled into one of the luxurious holes of the artillery boys. Captain Stout utilized another of the holes and Samsel another so we all settled down to a good night's sleep. Having plenty of spare time, the artillery crew members had really outdone themselves on those dugouts. First, they had dug a large hole three feet deep and covered it over with the wooden sides of ammunition boxes. After that they had mounded dirt over the roof and then camouflaged it with grass sod. Inside they had lined the bottom with a thick layer of dry hay. The constant rain made us extremely grateful for such a dry shelter, and I fell off into a deep sleep.

49

The next thing I remember I heard a loud hissing noise outside the hole and saw a blinding light outside the shelter half over the entrance. Following the noise was Lt. Stanchfield's voice saying, "Whose helmet is that? Man, it's really burned up!" Then I remembered that I had been careless enough to leave my helmet outside the tent flap and quickly popped my head out to see what had happened. George Samsel, an old artillery man, had been lecturing some of the men nearby on how the powder charges of a shell burn. He had told them the flames always go straight up in the air, so he lit one he found lying around for his proof. Unfortunately, he was badly mistaken, for the powder bag burst, showering burning powder for several yards. As luck would have it, one trail of powder had led right to my helmet lying in front of our hole.

Most GI's have the habit of carrying the toilet paper from K-rations in the top part of their helmets for two reasons: to have it handy for use and to keep it clean and dry. I had lined the top of my helmet with such paper, and when I looked at it I found the powder had touched off the paper, and the paper had kindled the leather head straps inside the helmet liner. Everyone had a big laugh out of it for a while until I remembered that we might be going into combat anytime soon, and the idea of combat without a helmet didn't appeal to me. Rather than go without, though, I readjusted the burned-out, stiff straps inside, so the helmet would at least seat itself on my head and offer some protection.

Towards noon that day we were ordered to pack up our things and get ready to move out. We all thought this would be it; but when I went ahead on the advance quartering party, I found we were just being moved to sleep in a large barn. The barn was located in the nearby small town of Beurig. The troops were to sleep in the hay loft with headquarters in two rooms downstairs. We really worked hard installing a stove in our room and getting other comforts fixed up for a comfortable night's sleep, but did we stay there? You guessed it - no! Instead, we packed up and moved back to our original positions at Irsch Hospital. We were told the reason was that the breakthrough threat had been stopped and our own forces had regained the lost territory. We were lucky enough to spend the next two nights in that hospital, though.

The last night in Irsch several of us were searching through some unused hospital buildings for more mattresses when we stumbled on three very attractive women in tight fitting OD sweaters. We couldn't help but stop where we were, and one fellow called out, "Look who's here!" Then another remarked, "Hello there, honey!" Out of a clear blue sky she answered back, "Hello yourself!" Then the other girl started speaking English, and we thought we were dreaming. It finally came out that they were all three officers in the army nurse corps and some General Hospital was thinking about setting up there. Man was I embarrassed!

When we left the hospital the second time we did go into combat. For the first few days we had a strictly holding position, but after that the real combat began. We moved out into some of the thickest evergreen woods I have ever seen and relieved another regiment of our own division. The woods were near Serrig, Germany, and we were on the western border of the well-known Rhine, Moselle, Saar triangle. Since the first platoon was far removed from the company CP, and I was still an aid man, I had to go out on line with the platoon.

The battalion CP was set up in a huge cave about three miles from the company, and the company CP was set up in a pill box (the outskirts of the Siegfried Line) about a half-mile from the first platoon. The first platoon CP was set up in a sunken water tank, which formed a sort of pill box. The men in the platoon were placed in well-constructed foxholes throughout the surrounding woods, for it had taken a suicidal attack by rangers to capture the position and we were to hold it at any cost. The rangers had lost several hundred men on their mission, which was easy to understand considering the terrain.

The platoon CP, as I mentioned before, was located in a large, buried concrete water reservoir which supplied water to the complex system of interlaced pill boxes and bunkers in that area. Its construction was similar to the pill boxes with its heavy steel door, and the part we lived in was a small valve room in the front part of the reservoir. The rest of the building was devoted to the two large concrete tanks, which still contained about a foot of water. Every time a shell struck near any of the pipes in the network branching out from our shelter, the concussion would travel up the pipes and crash against our ear drums in that re-echoing space.

To reach the valve room it was necessary to descend a set of stairs to a depth of about 12 feet below the level of the ground. Then one would find himself up against a small, solid steel door. Inside was the valve room measuring about three feet wide by 25 feet long. Naturally, it was cold and wet in the room at all times, but the sacrifice in comfort was worth the additional protection. Within our small CP we had a sound-power telephone connecting to a party line of six of our main outposts including two heavy machine guns from Dog Company. We also had an EE-8a (bell ringing) phone to the company CP and our second platoon, but we had to refrain from using the bell after dark because of the carrying power the sound had. We knew for sure the enemy was dug-in somewhere within 15 or 20 yards of us, and we didn't want to take any chances on tipping them off to our positions.

We were getting comfortably settled in our new home by the evening of the 12th, but at the same time we were getting nervous and uneasy. We weren't in too safe a position and were anxious to move on. In the Stars and Stripes newspaper we read about the First Army's lucky break at capturing the remaining bridge across the Rhine intact, and we knew that soon the entire American line would be moving forward to make its dash across the river along with the first. We weren't sure just when it would come, but we often spoke of it to pass the long hours of the day. While in the water tank, both Lt. Schmutz and I volunteered to take shifts on the telephones, and on the night of the 12th he had just come off duty and I had gone on when a whistle came over the company phone.

"Tell Lt. Schmutz to come down to the CP immediately. Captain Stout is on his way back from battalion and he wants to be sure and get all of the officers down there right away!" was all the voice said. I knew at that time of night it was no invitation to a social visit, so I woke up the lieutenant and gave him the message. He quickly started on his way, and as soon as he left I began wondering if this was it!

He was gone for four or five hours but I couldn't sleep and stayed right on the telephone. During the interim an enemy patrol got too close to one of our outposts, the men became panicky, and we finally repelled and wounded the intruders with a combination of grenades and machine gun fire.

Slightly after midnight, Lt. Schmutz stepped in the door. I looked at him for a minute, and even though he read the question in my eyes, all he said was the quiet command, "Get all of the squad leaders here right away! This is it!"

51

CHAPTER VIII

An air of stillness reigned over the small room after all the platoon non-coms had crowded in. Smoke clouded the atmosphere as each of the new arrivals, forbidden to smoke in their foxholes, inhaled their cigarettes. Finally, Lt. Schmutz began outlining the plan of attack in a low voice. The entire allied army was preparing to make a final drive to the Rhine. Behind our positions had been assembled one of the greatest artillery concentrations ever used; and between our lines and the artillery, the 80th Infantry Division had gone into position for a jump off. At 0300 one of the heaviest barrages ever used was to begin. After an hour and a half of shelling, the artillery was to lift and the 80th Infantry Division was to pass through our lines on the attack. Then we were to follow up and proceed to the flank of the other division.

I was somewhat relieved when I heard the plan, for at least we wouldn't have to make the initial assault. It was known by all of us that the woods to our front had been booby-trapped by both the German and American troops, and we felt better knowing that we wouldn't be the ones to clear them.

0300 came, and we all waited for the rumble of artillery to begin. Instead, silence persisted. We waited expectantly every minute of the next hour and a half, and finally at 0430 there was a deafening roar as scores of artillery pieces disgorged their deadly missiles. After the initial volley there was no slackening of intensity, and for 90 minutes the earth trembled for miles around. We became deaf in our water tank shelter from the constant re-echoing of shells striking the pipes, so I stepped outside to observe the pyrotechnic display.

To me it was a beautiful sight to watch the horizon glow with fire as each shell exploded, but I knew that what appeared beautiful to me was terrifying to unknown numbers on the receiving end. In the massive bombardment it was difficult to differentiate between the characteristic sounds of the 75mm. cannons, 105mm. howitzers, 155mm. rifles, 8-inch howitzers, 240mm. howitzers, 60mm. mortars, 80mm. mortars, and 4.2-inch chemical mortars; but I knew they were all there. Even the .30 and .50 caliber machine guns filled the air with their harassing tracers as every available type of weapon was used in an all-out psychological and physical attack against the enemy. Several of the artillery shells spread propaganda leaflets including a pink colored "surrender ticket" which entitled the bearer (with his comrades) to be taken prisoner and given all the rights granted him under the articles of the Geneva convention. Surprisingly enough, many of the Germans saved the official looking documents, and for several days we collected them from the "supermen" who solemnly declared, "Alles Kaput!"

After the barrage lifted we were disappointed to find the 80th Infantry Division did not pass through our woods. In fact, the closest they came to our position was a half-mile away, and we were left with the task of clearing out the rest of the enemy in front of us. Our terrific barrage, when ended, brought a feeble return from the enemy, but the shells were landing close enough to make our shelter inviting. The "incoming mail" also accomplished the task of destroying our communications with the company CP and the platoon outposts, but since we were leaving those positions I decided not to bother with repairing the breaks.

Captured German Nebelwerfer Rocket Launchers

This photo was taken by me near Hohenfurth, Czechoslovakia, one of several I took just as the war ended with a Zeiss Ikonta camera that I was able to purchase by lottery from the PX. It shows a field full of German rocket launchers (that we called "Screaming Meemies" because of the shrill and eerie sound they made while launching five rockets simultaneously) that were surrendered to our squad near the war's end, when German troops were scrambling to get away from advancing Russians, who were still seeking vengeance for the misdeeds of Germans marching towards Moscow earlier.
Photo by James Cutter; caption by James Cutter

At noon that day the rest of the platoons of our company were ordered to assemble at the first platoon CP and prepare for the attack. Waiting inside the water tank for this, I suddenly became aware of someone calling "Medic! Medic!" Scooping up my aid kits, I rushed outside and was directed down a column of men coming up from the company CP. Halfway down the path I discovered three men had been hit by screaming Meemies (Nebelwerfer Rockets). On the right side of the path, about five yards from where the shell had landed, I stopped to examine the first patient. I immediately saw he was past all medical aid, for he had died instantly when a shell fragment tore through the left side of his brain. Then I saw something I couldn't believe. On the other side of the path lay a

54

fellow I had thought was immune to shells after all the close shaves he had experienced. Not more than two yards from where the shell had landed lay Nagurney, the aid man with whom I had slept in Luxembourg and one of the oldest men with the company. His face was a pale yellow, and I was so surprised all I could say was, "My gosh, don't tell me they got you, Nag?"

"Yeah, those lousy Kraut ____!" was all he could reply. He wasn't too seriously wounded, but his entire right leg and part of his left were badly peppered with small perforating and penetrating wounds from the small pieces of shrapnel from the Nebelwerfer. He hadn't taken his morphine, so I gave him that first and then started on his legs. It was fortunate he had his aid kit there, for I used all the bandages he had on the countless wounds. I finally helped him onto a passing jeep and stared after him as he was carried away. I still couldn't believe Nag had been hit, and I couldn't expel the idea from my mind that perhaps it would be my turn next. Nag was a real aid man; and in spite of his six-and-a-half feet of height, he was the most fearless and carefree man in the medical section.

Rejoining my platoon, I found we had received orders to move out across the valley north of us and hold the next hill. Captain Stout had made a combat patrol out of us with the third platoon, and we were to go on ahead of the company. When we reached our objective, we were to radio back, and the remainder of the outfit would join us. We were assured the 80th Infantry Division had passed through the area, and we would meet no resistance; but I knew that was a lot of baloney. The 80th Infantry Division hadn't come anywhere near us. Also, if the job was so safe, why didn't the whole company come along at first instead of having to send back for them?

Having been out of direct combat for over a month, we were all nervous and scared stiff. None of us had felt the return of the old "combat nerves" yet, and every one of us, including Lt. Schmutz, hated the job ahead of us and feared it even more. We laughed and talked as the scouts went out ahead to clear our own mines, but as we began to follow after them I noticed an absolute silence. It was hot, and my breath came heavily from the unaccustomed exercise of running and dodging behind bushes in the open spaces. We passed a series of unused foxholes, and just as the head of the column rounded a turn, we hit the dirt as gun shots sounded up ahead. I really prayed that none of our men would get hit, for the idea of having to run up there to treat them drained away all of the steadiness I had managed to acquire. I trembled with the fear that someone would call, "Medic!", but my prayers were answered when a runner came trotting up the line of crouched men. He stopped when he came to Lt. Schmutz, and a few moments later the entire column turned around and proceeded back to our starting point, taking with us two prisoners.

Back at the water tank again I treated the wounded prisoners, and sometime later they informed us that there were two hundred enemy troops ahead of us! And the place was supposed to have been cleaned out! We considered ourselves lucky that the message from battalion to return had reached us in time; for an hour later the 80th Infantry Division did go through the area we were to take, and they had one of the fiercest fire fights I have ever witnessed just a little ahead of the point where we had stopped.

Realizing that we were one aid man short in case we should be called out for another attack, we radioed battalion for a replacement. The aid station had no idea Nag was hit, for he had been taken directly to regiment by the jeep driver. However, in a half hour Sgt. Curto arrived with our new aid man, Pfc. Benny Roddy. It was rather strange to have

Roddy back in Baker Company again, for he had started out originally with that organization last October. In November he was sent back to England with trench foot and was replaced by Nagurney. Now Nagurney had gone back to the hospital just as Roddy returned, so he was able to rejoin his old platoon again.

Just before dusk our orders were again changed, and we were told to proceed through the woods on the south and just ahead of us. Moving in that direction (with the first platoon out in front as usual) we discovered the forest was thick with Heinies in prepared positions, so we had to abandon the fight because of darkness. Once again, we returned to our water tank and spent another evening there.

By the next morning our nervousness had died down. Battalion sent down orders to move through the woods we had attempted the night before, stating that we were to leave at 0430. Realizing it would be suicidal to attempt it again in the darkness, we stalled around until daylight started breaking through. By that time battalion was demanding to know why we weren't on our way, and the messages over the radio were sharply punctuated with profanity. Once again Captain Stout chose the first platoon to do the dirty work alone, so with Leo (Doc) Wandyg (our first platoon sergeant) in the lead, we formed a long skirmish line and started cleaning out the woods. Remembering the many foxholes we had encountered before, we moved slowly and cautiously. Then we heard the loud report of a hand grenade and word passed down the line to me that Doc "got it." I raced up to treat him; but by the time I reached the spot, he had moved on with the attack.

Not until we were through cleaning out the woods would Doc let me treat him. He had been walking in the half-light of the early morning and had run into one of our own improvised booby traps, which consisted of a string across the path attached to a hand grenade in a tin can. As soon as Doc heard the pop of the cap on the grenade he knew what had happened, so he flopped on his stomach at the side of the path. He would have been safe if a log hadn't caught him in the pit of the stomach and held his tail end up in the air. When the grenade went off a small piece of shrapnel caught him right in the seat of the pants, but it didn't hurt so he continued on with the attack. I got him a purple heart for the wound, but he said he would never wear it. The embarrassment of explaining where he was hit would be too much for him.

I followed along with the platoon until we reached our objective; and, much to our surprise, we didn't encounter any resistance! When we were through and sitting down to rest, three Germans carrying a surrender propaganda leaflet and a large white flag walked in from behind us! After seeing they weren't going to be killed they told us they had been over in another section of the woods the night before when their company pulled out on the retreat. They had gotten together and decided they didn't wish to die for the Fatherland, so they went AWOL and waited for the Americans.

When the rest of the company caught up we proceeded on to where the other two companies of the battalion had stayed the night before. Because we had been delayed the night before we were made the reserve unit and were allowed to take off our equipment and relax in the holes already dug for us. I was just preparing to catch up on a little sleep when a wounded man from Charlie Company came limping out of the woods. He was only scratched up a little from shrapnel, so I bandaged him up. When I asked him how he got wounded he told me that his company had run into a mine field and all of the aid men were casualties. He said several of the men had their feet blown off and were without medical aid, so I grabbed my aid kits and took off for the mine field.

I didn't like the idea of going into any mine field for casualties, for we had always been taught not to take unnecessary risks. If we became a casualty ourselves going after another man we wouldn't do him or any of the other men any good. Nevertheless, something inside me kept me walking down that narrow path, and I soon came to the end of the column of men. They informed me the casualties were up at the head of the column, so I sent a man back for our company litter bearers. Finally, I reached the first casualty with a badly injured foot that would require amputation. He waved me on and said there were several worse casualties on up farther.

I soon realized this when I saw a group of three men lying together on the ground. The worst one had been bandaged up by one of the other medics before he became a casualty himself, but the aid man had neglected to put a tourniquet on the footless leg. As a result, the dressing had become saturated with blood, and the ground for several feet around was stained a bright red. I quickly applied one of my good rubber tourniquets (a captured souvenir from Saarlautern) on the leg and cut loose the old bandages. His foot had been removed from the ankle joint down with only a small piece of bone the size of a marble hanging on by a piece of skin. I knew that if I bandaged that up with the stump it would grate on the bone ends and cause him lots of unnecessary pain.

He had been administered morphine twenty minutes before and I hoped it had taken effect as I started to snip off the small strip of skin. I had just touched the flesh with my scissors when he jumped and withdrew the stump. Cold perspiration broke out all over my forehead and I felt sick at my stomach for a second or two. I wondered how the old-time surgeons ever managed to perform operations without an anesthetic. I left the leg as I had found it and padded the bone fragment to avoid friction. The tourniquet had stopped the flow of blood and the new dressing I put on remained fresh. The same fellow had been hit in the right eye with a particle from the mine, but outside of bandaging it up there was nothing else I could do for him. I later learned that he lost both his right leg and his right eye. His left leg had some bad powder burns and shrapnel holes in it, but they were able to save it.

The next fellow I treated had been hit in the foot and thigh. I patched him up and turned to one of the aid men they had just brought up to me on a litter. Two of his toes on his left foot had been blown loose and he had multiple shrapnel wounds and burns all over his body. The other aid man, Mitchell, wasn't wounded as severely and returned from the hospital just after the war ended in time to take my place as aid man with Company B.

The rest of the men I treated I don't remember, but there were seven or eight casualties altogether. Two or three lost limbs, and Mitchell came out of it the lightest of all. When I finished with Charlie Company, Lipson, another aid man from Baker Company, came up with the story that Company A had also run into a mine field and lost all of their medics. I was exhausted - both mentally and physically - but I refilled my aid kits from the wounded medics' bags and started for the other company.

En route to the other unit Lipson and I discovered a wounded engineer from a mine clearing team. Part of his foot had been blown off by a mine, so we hastily dressed it and proceeded on. We finally reached the Able Company CP, but the men stationed there said they didn't have any idea where the mine field was. They told us the company had just left the six or seven casualties lying where they had fallen and had gone on. For two hours we tried to locate the wounded men without success. Finally, we returned to our own CP to see if anything new had come up. At the company we met Curto with some litter bearers and a new crew of engineers. Once again, we set out in search for the wounded, and again had no results. Upon returning to Baker Company we discovered they were preparing to move out again, so we left Curto and his men and returned to our platoons. In the preceding 24 hours our battalion had lost 2/3rds. (8 out of 12) of its aid men, so we were really shorthanded.

A week later I found out that no one had been able to locate the A Company mine field until three days later, when some TD (tank destroyer) men passed through there and found them. Robinson, the medic with whom I had slept in Luxembourg, was the only aid man left; and he had managed to keep three other men alive. His left leg and arm were blown off and had to be completely amputated. He was in such a state of combat exhaustion that it was doubted whether he would live. How he managed to live through those three torturous days and nights in his condition is still a wonder to me, for he was always a highly strung and meek fellow.

Baker Company by-passed the mine fields and pulled up next to a chateau in the middle of a large woods. A heavy barrage of mortar shells was falling all around us, but luckily, they didn't produce any casualties. Charlie and Able Companies were out in front of us with a large gap in between them, and our mission was to fill in and protect against a possible counter-attack. That sounded like anything but inviting to me, for the heaviest concentration of shells was landing right in the area where we were to go. We waited around for about an hour with the mortars still going, and we began to wonder where they were getting all the ammunition and whether they would ever cease. Finally, Captain Stout sent a combat patrol from the first platoon into the gap between the two companies to see what was there. The first thing they ran into was a hidden machine gun, which couldn't be spotted because of the falling darkness. Then the message came that the company on the left had withdrawn so we pulled back to the chateau and awaited orders.

Leading out from the front door of the chateau was a large gravel highway. This seemed strange to us, for it apparently led nowhere, however, it looked like a good route for a counter attack, so we placed anti-tank mines and machine guns out to protect it. Then we sat around and waited until ten o'clock, when the order was issued that we had to proceed on to our objective at all costs that night. It seemed that the highway was urgently needed for our tanks to come up on, but since we hadn't seen any friendly tanks for several days and they were worthless in the woods, we couldn't see the big rush. At any rate, we moved out the next morning at 0300 in what seemed like an absolutely suicidal attack in that pitch-blackness

That night everyone was jittery. Lt. Schmutz was called off the line for a pass to Paris, and our platoon was left without a leader. Just the same, Captain Stout made our first platoon the spearhead for the attack and stuck us out in front as usual. The only other lieutenant in the company was new and scared to death so he stuck to the rear. Holding on to each others' belts to avoid being separated, we silently followed up the edge of the woods past the German positions. We felt sure that we were walking right into an ambush, for we had seen enemy troops in that woods just a few hours before.

Moving slowly so as to avoid making any sounds, we finally came to the road junction of the large road leading from the chateau with a small cross-road, just as it was getting light. We stopped and held our breath, though, for just ahead we heard the clinking noise of what sounded like the enemy digging in. After a while it stopped, so Paridis, one of our best squad leaders, went up where it had come from and threw a few grenades. Then he went to the four corners of the cross-roads and tossed grenades without any reply. To our complete surprise he found an elaborate pill box on one of the corners, and the sounds we had heard were those made by the former occupants in evacuating it. After a thorough search we found the structure to be empty of both personnel and mines, so the first platoon was given a break and left to guard the fortification while the rest of the company went on.

I had seen the pill boxes of the Maginot Line before, but I had never had the opportunity to carefully examine one of the Siegfried Line. It consisted of two levels, the bottom floor being devoted to sleeping quarters and the top to a machine gun position. It was really more of a bunker than a pill box, for it could sleep about two dozen men. I imagine the personnel who manned that concealed machine gun we ran into the night before had come from the bunker, and they probably supplied men to many of the adjacent pill boxes. The inside of the bunker was elaborately equipped with bunks, electricity, running water, and a telephone. The outside walls were several feet thick, and none of the doors or halls led directly into any of the rooms. Instead, there was a zigzag hallway with small holes through the walls so anyone entering the hallway could be eliminated before getting too far. This hall system also eliminated any possibility of throwing grenades in on the occupants. All of the doors had heavy wing bolts on them, so the men inside could securely fasten them and fire out through ports. The machine gun position was connected with the sleeping quarters by a speaking tube only so that even if one room were captured the others could still fight.

The first thing we did in our new home was to start looting. I found a double-barreled signal pistol with a complete set of flares, evidently used for signaling the other pill boxes in case the communications were knocked out. I also discovered a German flashlight with a built-in generator, making batteries unnecessary. All you had to do was to keep clenching your fist for a steady light. I also found a good Norwegian-made hunting knife that I carried thereafter. I discovered an SS trouper's cap, which I intended to keep for a souvenir; but a lieutenant from Company D said he had found it first so I let him have it. There were plenty of rations there, but since I don't care for limburger cheese or their tough crackers, I left them alone. At 0900 I decided to try to catch up on the sleep I had lost the evening before and was just sprawling out on one of the beds when Col. Gladding showed up and told us we were relieved. The battalion CP was going to use the pill box for its shelter, so we had to move out and rejoin the company.

The Dog Company lieutenant was briefly oriented on how to get up to Baker Company, so we started out again. Halfway up there we started receiving 88 fire. Since we were in the middle of a large woods and they were all tree bursts, Paridis tried to get the officer to stop and lay low until the barrage was over; but he refused. Then, up at the end of the column, I heard the call, "Medic!" Running all the way up to the front, I found the lieutenant had been hit by shrapnel, and as I started to work on him he died in my arms. The shrapnel had pierced his left side and gone through his heart and lungs, so he died almost instantly. The strange part of it all was that Paridis was leading the column and the shell had landed in a tree in front of him. The lieutenant, who was right behind Paridis, was killed; and Paridis wasn't even scratched!

After a while the barrage ended so we went on using what little information the lieutenant had given Paridis. Luckily (and most of that luck was due to Paridis's exceptional leadership and 100% backing of his men) we reached the company without getting lost. They were being held up by another enemy fortified position and had requested artillery fire on it. The artillery refused us, so we had to by-pass the concealed machine gun. The rest of that day was uneventful and consisted of hiking about ten more miles without meeting any resistance.

That evening we had hoped to get a little rest, but as usual the battalion ordered us on to another new objective. We kept going until sometime in the early morning, when we dug-in in a small patch of woods next to an enemy artillery ammo dump. During the night an enemy ammunition detail, not suspecting our presence, sauntered down to the dump for shells and were very much surprised to be taken prisoners.

The next morning, we found out that battalion had wished us to keep going all night long, and only the human understanding of Captain Stout had allowed us to stop and catch a few hours sleep. However, he received a real chewing out for it and was threatened with a court martial if he ever did it again! All that morning we kept finding fresh foot prints and tank tracks in the mud but no enemy in sight.

Around 1000 that day we came across a large gravel highway; and after following it for several hundred yards, we connected up with two companies of the 101st Infantry Regiment. They had captured two German jeeps and a large truck and had left them upright on the road as they had found them. That was where they made their mistake and what was the cause for one of the closest calls I had in the entire war.

There we were: all three companies standing out in plain sight on the road next to the vehicles when two of our own P-47's started circling overhead. We didn't pay any attention to them and supposed them to be friendly. Then some fools jumped in the vehicles and tried to move them into the woods. That's all the pilots needed, and all I can remember now is hearing the loud roar of a diving plane and someone yelling, "Hit It!" I dove for the left side of the road and started trembling worse than I have ever done before. Then I heard the popping of the machine guns and saw the dirt flying alongside of me where the bullets were hitting.

The next thing I knew I was flung aside and my ears rang from the bomb which landed only 50 yards to my left and uprooted a large tree. I was whole so far, but when I heard the second plane starting to dive I knew the jig was up. I can't describe the helplessness I felt lying there: I knew for sure the next bomb would get me, for I was lying between the first bomb and the one truck left on the highway. This time the bullets were no closer, but the bomb landed only 35 yards to my left, lifted me off the ground, and sprayed me with dirt and rocks. Well, the first two bombs had missed, but they were gradually working closer. I felt sure when they circled for the next attempt that they would get me.

I realized that I had run to the wrong side of the road, so I used that time to run across to the heavy woods on the right side of the road. By that time one of the radio men had gotten through to battalion, battalion had contacted regiment, regiment had contacted division, division had notified air-ground control, and they in turn had radioed the pilots. I trembled for almost an hour after that experience for it really was the closest call and most terrifying experience I have ever had. Fortunately, our company didn't have any casualties; but the 101st Infantry Regiment had one fellow killed and several wounded.

We went on again and that afternoon met up with Charlie Company, who followed along with us for the rest of the afternoon. Our platoon (still without an officer) was leading as usual when we came upon a German tank. We didn't know whether or not they had seen us, so we tried a surprise attack on them. Several of the men from our platoon (led by Doc

Wandyg) crawled up to the tank, and just as they were about to enter it some half-wit in Charlie Company cut loose with a bazooka. Luckily none of our men were hurt, but it spoiled the surprise element, so force had to be used. Doc hopped on top of the vehicle, which apparently had stopped in the woods to hide from our planes and pulled the Krauts out. Then he jumped inside to see what he could find in the way of souvenirs. That's the way Doc always was, and I've seen him take a town just to get bread and jam out of the cellars of the houses. We took three SS tankers prisoner, and Doc came out of it all with a pair of binoculars.

A little later on that day our company got lost and entered a valley it didn't belong in. As a result, we received a hail of machine gun fire from enemy troops we couldn't see. Our men deployed along the sides of both hills, and after a terrific fire fight we decided we'd better get back to our own route and leave that mess to the second battalion. We were starting to leave when someone missed Lucky Newman, and we started a search for him. We found him after a while with a sniper's bullet through his brain. I could hardly believe it, for Lucky had really been everyone's friend and had amused us for hours back in Guerlfangen with his organ music.

That evening I was running low on medical supplies, so I went back to the aid station. Staying there two nights, I was able to make a deal concerning my staying on as an aid man. I had just about forgotten the idea of going back to the infantry since it was taking so long, so Sgt. Curto and the captain talked me into remaining with the medics by waving a T/3 (Technical rank equivalent to staff Sergeant) in my face. After some discussion, I had the transfer canceled and settled down to hope for a quick ending to the war.

The night I left the company had been our last day of extensive hiking. The companies had broken through the last thick woods and the 11th Armored Division had taken over the attack in a whirlwind chase of the disorganized Germans. For the next few days and up until we crossed the Rhine on March 24, we took anywhere from 12 to 20 towns a day and rode on tanks and trucks to keep up. Our company would generally start out on foot to capture the first town or two for the day. Once we had gotten the Heinies running we would hop on tanks and chase them even faster. If we came to a town that looked as if it had some kind of defense, we would hop off the tanks and form a huge battalion-size skirmish line. Then, walking upright, everyone would fire his weapon from the hip into town. The heavy machine guns would set up behind us and fire over our heads if possible. The tanks would spray all the buildings with machine gun fire and blast any sniper hide-outs. When over five hundred weapons are fired all together and just as fast as possible, it makes enough noise to scare anyone to death, so usually the Germans surrendered. If not, we would search every house and fire through every window in town. That system really got results with the least expenditure of men on our part.

On March 23, our battalion moved into a large field and bivouacked there preparatory to crossing the Rhine. The crossing of that river had always held fear in our hearts, for it was expected the enemy would put up a last ditch stand there at the last natural obstacle to Germany. We had been assured it would be a fierce and bloody battle getting across and would be similar to the Normandy beach landing on June 6, 1944. We didn't know just how close to the river we were, but all that night and the next day the sky to the east of us was filled with exploding anti-aircraft fire and yellow flares.

After sunset on the 24th, our officers were called to battalion headquarters for a meeting of utmost importance and secrecy. When they returned I overheard two of them whispering. One of the officers said, "Well, this is it! We're going to cross tonight!" Not knowing that a crossing had already been made and two pontoon bridges erected, we all expected to make an amphibious assault landing with a large artillery barrage softening up the defenses for us. Instead, we were later informed, the Third Army had made a surprise crossing without even a shot being fired and our two bridges were handling every kind of military traffic. In the day time the bridges were entirely hidden by smoke screens, but at night darkness was the only cover. For 24 hours a day German planes would fly over and try to destroy the installation, and just that day seven of the enemy aircraft had been shot down.

The moon was shining brightly that night as we loaded onto the tanks that were to transport us across. We were five miles from the Rhine, and the original plan had been for the troops to walk across on the southernmost bridge. At the last minute, though, Colonel Gladding had consented to our riding on the tanks instead. When we reached the approaches of the bridge there was a heavy stream of traffic lined up to cross ahead of us, and the problem of supply was so great the bridge had been declared one-way except for one hour in the morning. In other words, once we were across there would be no getting back for several weeks unless we were wounded or had some other high priority.

At 2330 that night our column began to move, and our lead tank mashed the first pontoon of the bridge deeply into the water as it started across. Except for the loud roar of the tanks' engines, everything was still; and we all prayed the Germans wouldn't pick that time to try to bomb us. If such a thing did happen, our orders were clear: We were to keep on moving and the flow of vehicles was not to slow down even for a second.

Reaching the east bank of the Rhine safely, we turned southward to catch up with the fourth armored division. Our mission was to proceed along with them and help guard their exposed southern flank from being cut off by a counter attack.

Everyone was happy to be back with the fourth armored again, for praises were mutual between the two divisions after the action we had seen together in Lorraine the preceding Fall. In fact, the armored division had stated that we were the only division that could keep up with them and had requested our presence on several different occasions. We received a royal welcome from the old fourth armored boys that night when we pulled up to them, and a series of bull sessions about old times sprang up right away. They told us it gave them a much safer feeling to have the YD along protecting them, and we assured them that it gave us an even better feeling to know at last we were back with the one armored outfit that wouldn't pull back and leave us when the going got too rough.

That night we dug-in beside the forward elements of the other division just outside a fiercely burning town. With all their heavy armor and fire power, an armored division doesn't have to take any chances when capturing a city. They generally pull up into position just outside the place, blast everything in sight, and ask questions later. I am firmly convinced that is the way a modern war should be fought, even though it is rather hard on the civilians. After all, they are just as much responsible for the war as their soldiers; and if they have so much time and money to spend on war, then they can afford to use the same for building new homes. Using the armored's system makes casualties almost negligible, for the German soldiers that aren't killed soon surrender.

The next morning, we loaded onto trucks and followed up the point of one of the spearheads of the attack. To everyone's surprise a huge German ammunition dump was captured intact, but it was all wired with demolitions and no one knew where the switch was. The dump was spread out in a large forest and was one of the largest I have ever seen. It was so cleverly camouflaged that even the main highways and railroad tracks leading into it looked as if they passed right on through an innocent woods from the air. Our engineers were afraid to cut any of the demolitions wires for fear of a double-back circuit which would detonate the entire dump and level everything for miles around. Our battalion's job for that day and night was guarding the dump, for we all knew it was a prize the Krauts would try to get back. Fortunately, though, no counter attack developed, and we moved on in pursuit of the fourth armored the next day.

The Main River was the dividing line between the Third and Seventh Armies at that time, but the Seventh Army had just made a small beach head across the Rhine and was 100 miles behind us. The fourth armored had made a lucky capture and taken a long double railroad bridge across the Main river near Kahl-am-Main. The bridge had been prepared for demolition with large bombs, but for some reason only one span of one of the two parallel bridges had been destroyed. We arrived the next morning and found that a suicide squad of Germans had tried to crawl up to the bridge with demolition charges the night before, but they had been discovered and the ensuing fire fight set off some of the charges the men were carrying. Lying in the middle of the field below was the hairy scalp of one of the attempted saboteurs with his headless body over a hundred yards away. Several other barely recognizable bodies lay even closer to the tracks.

Our job was to hold the bridge at all costs until we were relieved by the Seventh Army. It was anything but a comfortable feeling to be there, for we knew the Germans had a large force in the next town and we were only a battalion in strength. In fact, when the Seventh Army did relieve us it took a whole division a week to clean out the next town, for it was filled with several thousand fanatical SS troops. Fortunately, we didn't know it was that bad at the time or we never would have gotten any sleep.

As had been the custom for the past month or two, Steve (Stephens), Hambrick, and I started digging in together. Then we noticed several large boat houses down by the river and started investigating. Evidently it had been a German amphibious landing school, for it was completely equipped with landing barges, huge Blitzkrieg (lightning war) engines, and schools for classes in tactics and mechanics. We picked up several long-handled shovels to make our digging easier and then noticed an elaborate carbide signal lantern, which we took along for reading that night if we could blackout our hole. It was a beautiful lantern made entirely of brass and unlike any other carbide lamp I had ever seen before. It was evidently used on the barges for long periods of time to provide a water proof signal light, for it came in a case complete with red, blue, amber, and green lenses and black-out shutters.

Just as we returned to our hole the order came down for Hambrick and Steve to report to the CP. There they found out they had to make a reconnaissance into the next town. The orders stated they were to walk into the city as far as they could until they drew enemy fire, and then they were to report what they had seen. It was the most crazy mission I had ever heard of, but to Steve and Hambrick, experienced veterans of patrol work, it was just another assignment, so they went on. Stopping on the hill at the edge of the city, they couldn't see any traces of the enemy, but they could tell the city was large enough to merit Captain Stout's suggestion that they take along four or five men.

They reported back to him and found that Lipson, the German linguist for the company as well as aid man, wanted to go along to question the civilians. They also took Doc Wandyg along; for, as usual, he had already been into one of the houses on the outskirts of town for bread and jam. One or two other riflemen went along, and Lipson traded his brassard for an M-l rifle. I hated to see them leave, but they started off in good spirits, joking about how much loot they were going to get. When they disappeared out of sight I returned to the job of digging our three-man foxhole, for I felt I had to have something to keep me busy.

A half-hour later I heard the sound of a rapid-fire M-l and knew that only three men could make a rifle talk that fast. Those three men were Paridis (who was on pass to Paris), Doc Wandyg, and Steve. Paridis had the record on fast shooting, though, for when he fired his rifle it sounded just like a machine gun with only eight shots. Steve ran a close second behind Paridis, and Doc almost tied with Steve. None of those three men would ever fire just one shot. They would always empty a clip of eight if they were going to fire at all, for it only took them the same amount of time to fire eight shots as it took the normal man to fire one.

I knew by the sound that came back to me that the patrol had run into trouble, but I felt sure they could take care of themselves. A few minutes later all the men came running back but Steve, and when Doc could get his breath he gasped, "They got Steve!" I couldn't believe it, for Steve had always led a charmed life. Doc told me they had tried to reach him to see if he was dead, but the hail of lead had been too much for them. Hambrick had gone back for a jeep, and a short while later they returned with Steve's body.

Everyone was quiet that afternoon, but finally Doc came out with the story of what had happened. They had gotten into the town without receiving any enemy fire. A BAR (Browning Automatic Rifle) team was stationed in one of the first houses to cover any hasty retreat they might have to make, and Steve, Doc, Hambrick, and Lipson had gone on. A little farther in the town they received a great deal of sniper fire, so they ducked into one of the houses, where they were safe from the small arms and could have waited all day without being harmed. Lipson became scared and began shouting, "They're coming, they're coming! We're surrounded, we're surrounded!" Then he ran out the door to make a break for it. The others followed behind with Steve in the rear. Steve decided to investigate the shots and was delayed a little longer than the rest but when he tried to catch up with them he was shot in the back by a sniper.

That day Lt. Schmutz returned from Paris to be greeted by the sad news of the loss of his platoon guide. None of us felt like talking so we just worked up until darkness on our foxhole. It was an elaborate affair tunneled into the embankment of a highway. The sloping front was covered with heavy railroad ties for both protection and black-out. Then we covered the bare wood with strips of sod so as to camouflage it. With a shelter half over the doorway and straw to sleep on we really had a cozy little place, but neither Hambrick nor I felt right with Steve absent from his usual place in the middle of the three-man bed.

The next morning everything went along as usual until we saw two men walking down the road from town. As they came closer we recognized them as Doc and Russel, his assistant squad leader. No one had missed either of the two men, and none of us had any idea where they had been. They stopped at my hole. Doc was holding up a brand-new stop watch, and Russel was wearing a new pair of German binoculars around his neck. I knew then that they had been into town again and had gone with the sole mission of avenging Steve's death. Doc chuckled, "Well, we got the one bastard for sure, and I think we got another one!" Then he related how they had gone up beside the barn from where the shots had come the day before. They discovered a German soldier sleeping beside the hay pile; and Doc whispered to Russel, "When you shoot him, don't hit him in the arm or hip because he might have a watch!" Then both men cut loose with eight shots and nearly cut him in two. Russel got his binoculars and Doc found the stop watch, still in its new box, in the fellow's pocket. Of course, Doc stopped on his way back and picked up some bread and jam for all of us.

That afternoon we were relieved by elements of the Seventh Army and returned to the other bank of the Main River. We had a great deal of fun there with two little motorcycles we found in the garage of the house the CP stayed in. While riding down one of the roads, some of the men discovered a German supply parachute dump, where huge silk parachutes colored a bright red were packed in bomb-like containers for use in dropping supplies to cut-off ground troops. That night many of us slept in comfort in our foxholes lined with brilliant red silk!

The next day our company was in reserve for a change, so we road in large two-and-a-half ton trucks and followed the other two companies, who were pursuing the Krauts in trucks. Everything went smoothly until the two lead companies tried to take a town that was heavily protected. They managed to capture several prisoners, so they sent them back to us to get them off their hands. One of the Krauts had worked for the Ford Motor Company in Shanghai for 17 years and spoke perfect English. There was no trace of accent (other than English) in his diction, and we spent an enjoyable two hours with him discussing the war and the attitude of the Germans. He reassured us that if it had been up to the Wehrmacht (regular army, in contrast with SS), the war would have been over a month before; and he insisted that only the SS and officers were continuing the fight. That was the 31st of March, and he predicted the war wouldn't last another month: but he missed it by a week.

While we were waiting at the outskirts of the town we were all terrified for a moment by a strangely unfamiliar roaring noise in the air overhead. Then we heard the familiar popping of .50 caliber bullets, so we hit it for the woods. Later we found out it had just been a German jet-propulsion plane with our own ack-ack firing at it. So far that is the first and only time I have seen a jet plane.

Around five o'clock that afternoon the other two companies withdrew from the town after discovering it was another regiment's area. Our company was given the task of clearing out snipers from the woods on the edge of town and then following up a main highway to a town about seven miles away. Our first platoon started out in the lead, but just as it was getting dark our route of attack was changed. So, Captain Stout had the third platoon by-pass us on the new route. That relieved my mind a great deal, for that was another of those coal-black, jittery evenings.

We kept walking and walking until most of us were doing it in our sleep, when finally, the column stopped. Immediately most of us slumped over to the side of the road and leaned up against the steep terrace which led into a dense forest. I had just reached the bend of the road, so it was impossible for me to determine what was happening up ahead.

100 yards to our right, at the foot of a steep hill about 75 feet high, was a railroad track; and on the other side of the tracks was another large hill. On that opposite hill we could hear German vehicles moving and men's voices as they worked, apparently unaware of our presence. A moment before we halted, Lt. Schmutz said he heard someone up ahead run down the bank and across the valley towards the sounds of voices, but no one else had heard it.

We were all resting there beside the road when all hell broke loose without any warning! First, I heard and saw the flash of a grenade exploding in the middle of the road less than ten yards up ahead. The noise had just succeeded in bringing me to my senses when one of the "super-fast" German burp guns started spraying the road and both sides. Seeing that the fire originated from the same spot as the grenade, I immediately flattened out but found there was no ditch to provide cover. Then I tried climbing the bank, but when I got halfway up I saw tracers shooting through the trunks of the trees just above my hands. Deciding I was better off in my original position, I slid down and took the prone again.

By that time the firing had ceased so I started looking for casualties. Lipson came up to me excited and out of breath panting, "Cutter, one of my fellows got hit and the guys all think he's dead, but he's lying right up at the machine gun. What am I going to do?" That was the last straw! He, an aid man, knew his job and he had the nerve to come to me and ask me what to do! Immediately several suggestions of what he might do (although unrelated to the case at hand) popped into my head, and just as I was getting ready to escort him up to the casualty, one of the men in my platoon came up with the news that "Phil" (T/4 Phillips) had been hit. I quickly dispensed with Lipson by telling him that he would have to go on up to his man if he could possibly make it and not take any unnecessary chances. Later Lipson told me he examined the fellow, but when we tried to locate the body he didn't have any idea where it was.

I couldn't believe that Phil, one of the quietest and most intelligent fellows in the platoon, had been hit until I saw him. He had been wounded in the arms and left side by the initial machine gun burst but had walked back about 50 feet to a safe place before telling anyone he had been hit. I knew his consideration had been for my safety, but unfortunately, he had been two men in front of me when he was wounded and had taken all those unnecessary steps for nothing. When I reached him, he was in great pain but not bleeding too seriously. He was one of the bravest patients I have ever had, and even though he was on the verge of unconsciousness from the intense pain, he never let on to me that it bothered him. He thought the entire length of his arm had been perforated by bullets; but after a crude examination in the total darkness, Roddy and I could find only one hole, just above the elbow. By feeling the holes made by the bullets passing through his side I could determine that it had probably pierced his kidneys, so it would be necessary to evacuate him immediately to control the internal hemorrhages. We laid him on a litter and I told the bearers to get him to the aid station as soon as possible.

The next day I found out that even the colonel didn't know where he had put the battalion aid station, so they put Phil on a jeep and started looking for it. Three hours later they discovered it. Two days later we learned that Phil had died en route to the hospital from the aid station. I have always blamed the station for that death until just recently, when I looked up the records and discovered they were following orders all that night. There was no reason why the battalion headquarters didn't know the station's location, for

66

they had placed the medics in the house where they were set up. At any rate, it doesn't do any good afterwards to try to place the blame for someone's death after he is already gone.

After some investigation I discovered what had caused all the trouble that night. The enemy had constructed a large road block with three foxholes on the edges of the road to guard it. They had blown out a large section of the pavement and placed fallen trees across the road between the excavation and the foxholes. One hole contained the machine gunners, and the hole opposite it sheltered the men who threw the grenade. The third hole was unoccupied at that time, so we took it for granted that those were the men Lt. Schmutz had heard departing earlier in the night. Evidently the third platoon (which was leading the attack) had surprised them, for in the darkness all but two or three of their men had passed the machine gun. Since our platoon was following the third, the machine gun had opened up on the bulk of our boys. After the first few bursts the machine gun had jammed so our men seized the opportunity to capture the gunners. Altogether we took three young prisoners that night and three more plus an officer the next day.

The colonel finally caught up to us with his tanks and supporting company, so we just stood around and waited for orders. He called for engineers to remove the road block, but long before they arrived he sent the first platoon on to the next town, which had already been taken by another company. The only way around the road block was to follow the railroad tracks, but just as soon as we got the entire platoon down the bank some hidden Kraut fired a Panzerfaust (the German version of our bazooka anti-tank weapon) at us. Luckily no one was injured, so we returned to the company for reorganization. This time Lt. Schmutz decided to take only two squads with him, so I was left behind with the one remaining squad. That night the rest of the platoon accomplished their mission without any mishaps and stayed all night in the next town. Lipson and I spent the rest of the night curled up under one blanket, for we were given orders not to break down our packs because we might move out any time.

The next morning, Easter Sunday, April Fool's Day, and the first day of my second year in the army combined, found us still waiting for the engineers. They finally arrived shortly after daybreak and enlisted the help of our prisoners to fill in the crater. We were all walking around without any concern, and we all examined the machine gun and holes that had caused us all the trouble the proceeding night. They had been dug-in right next to the edge of the steep bank that led down to the tracks. Nearby was a house from which an old frau came to plead for her son, who was one of our prisoners. We sent her right back to the house and assured her we wouldn't harm her son. About a thousand yards away was a town that had not been taken yet, and we all grew uneasy as we heard a self-propelled gun maneuvering around in that distant village. However, when it failed to fire at us we forgot about it.

I was just starting to heat up a cup of coffee when I heard a sharp crack that a bullet makes when it penetrates something nearby. I looked up in a hurry to see where it had come from; but since I never heard the report of the rifle I supposed it was just a long-range sniper from the town. Then I heard someone call, "Medic! Hey, Cutter!" I set the coffee down and grabbed my aid kit. Then I heard the same voice tell me, "Samsel got hit!" I still couldn't locate the source of the voice; but I saw everyone near the foxholes taking cover, so I decided the trouble must be there.

When I arrived at the former machine gun position, I found that Rogers, the second platoon runner and one of my close friends from Saarlautern, had been calling me. He had nearly lost his self-control from the excitement but from what he told me I pieced out the story of what had happened. He and Samsel had been examining the foxholes (as the rest of us had done) when he heard the loud crack and saw Samsel sort of freeze for a second and then tumble forward down the steep embankment. Schwarz, one of our company litter bearers, had already gone down to him so I hurried after.

George hadn't rolled as far as the tracks yet, but when I reached him he was in a bad state of shock. His face was a yellowish-white, and when I saw him I knew he couldn't live. But I was determined to do everything possible in my power to make the going easier for him and still try to save him. The bullet had entered his right side just under the arm; and from the direction it was traveling, if it had gone far enough, it had probably lodged in his heart. It was evident that it had gone through one of his lungs and possibly his kidney. He halfway recognized me, but the stare in his eyes dominated his spirit, and he became hysterical. I immediately gave him morphine to try to ease the pain and get him out of shock, but he kept trying to move around. I hurriedly bandaged up his side and helped load him on a litter. By that time, it became apparent that he would never make it.

The litter bearers carried him to a jeep, but he passed away en route to the aid station. All that day I couldn't help but think of how he used to kid me in Saarlautern about how he wanted me to take care of him if he ever got wounded, and when he finally did get it I was helpless.

That afternoon we all loaded onto trucks and rode about 20 miles up to some more territory the fourth armored had taken which was in the Seventh Army's zone. Colonel Gladding decided that he would send his tanks on into the next large town just on the other side of where the armored division had stopped. Then the rest of us (in the same convoy of vehicles and right behind the tanks) would follow on into town.

When we reached the hill just before the city, most of the column pulled into a large field and waited for the all clear signal. The tanks had just started in when an 88-shell landed right in the middle of the field we were in. I don't know whether it was cowardliness or just concern for their vehicles, but the drivers had us unloaded and had started back up the road before the next shell could land! Of course, the tanks pulled back and left the infantry with the problem of taking the town! Because we had taken such a beating the night before, our company was in reserve and told to dig in on the reverse slope of the hill on the edge of town. Captain Stout, pitying us for once, told the first platoon it could be in company reserve and dig in on the top of the second hill from town. Since we had already started our holes in front of the rest of the company we were griped to say the least.

We started digging in our new position when a German 105 or 150 mm. shell landed about 100 yards behind us. That was too close for me, and in this new position we didn't have any hill to protect us. Several of us suggested to Lt. Schmutz that we return to our old holes where we were at least protected from artillery. He flatly refused, saying, "Our orders are to dig in here, so we'll just have to sweat it out." I knew he wasn't convinced, though, so when the second shell landed a little closer we repeated our suggestion. That time he half-conceded to our idea but still chose to follow the order. The third shell burst was too close, so he threw down his shovel and shouted, "to hell with it! Come on, men, let's go back!" We didn't need any second invitation and quickly gathered up our equipment and ran. Just as we reached our original positions, another shell landed right in the middle of where we had been standing!

Able and Charlie Companies stayed in the half-taken town that night, so we felt fairly safe from a counter-attack. Tex's squad was sent out about 700 yards away from us to guard the eastern approach to the town, and battalion set up its CP in the village behind us. That night passed without any trouble from the enemy, but by morning a dismal, all-day rain had begun. Being near battalion, we were forced to remain out in our holes; but Tex's squad took advantage of their distant outpost position and moved into a nearby house. We all envied them until that night.

Doc Wandyg started out on his never-ending search for food that evening by accompanying the runner from the outpost squad back to the house they had taken over. Glen Williams, my foxhole partner, and I were the only ones who knew about his departure; but knowing Doc, we were sure he could take care of himself. An hour later a runner from the outpost group hurried up to me and spit out, "Cutter, Tex got it - he's dead!" I still hadn't fully recovered from Steve's, Phillips's and Samsel's deaths, so that news was about all I could take.

Then the runner continued with his story. When Doc arrived at the house all the men gathered around him, leaving no one on guard outside. Then after Doc and two other men had departed, Tex suddenly realized that no one was outside, and it was getting dark. He volunteered to stand guard and had only been outside a few minutes when the rest of the men heard a shot. Going outside, they found Tex, pistol in hand, lying right on his face with a bullet through the back of his head. He was near the corner of the building, so they knew the shot must have come from close range and evidently from the pistol of someone standing up on the back porch of the house. They shuddered to think what would have happened if Tex had not surprised the intruder, for one grenade in the room would have probably gotten all of them.

After hearing his story, I sent the litter bearers back with him to carry the body to the company. The runner had received some long-range sniper fire on his way up to the company, but he had to return to recover the body and instruct the rest of the men to move out of the house.

An hour later Doc Wandyg and the other two men he had taken with him on his quest for food returned to the company. He stopped first at my hole and to my horror told me that he had returned to the house where they had stayed that day and had found it completely deserted. The squad was long overdue, so the first thing that popped into my mind was that they had been captured. Doc didn't know about Tex's death but said he had found a puddle of blood in the house. When he had reached the building it was entirely dark, and when he examined the interior he found it to be empty.

We talked it over for a while and then decided the best thing to do was tell the CO about it so he could send out a patrol to hunt for the missing men. Just as I reached Captain Stout's hole the rest of the men in Tex's squad came marching down the road. I was so relieved I couldn't get mad at them; for, since Glen and I had been the only ones who knew anything about what was going on, we really felt responsible for the entire group. I soon learned that Tex's burden had slowed them down and they had received more sniper fire, causing them to change their route. So that accounted for their slowness in reaching the company. It was well after midnight before I got to bed that night, but I was so keyed up it was impossible to sleep.

The next day we were relieved by a cavalry outfit from the Seventh Army. When we marched back to the town where battalion was set up, we discovered half of the houses and barns in flames. Some sniper hidden in one of the houses had wounded one of our men, so the colonel tossed a couple of white phosphorus grenades in some of the surrounding houses that he could have been concealed in. As a result, half of the town had caught on fire and was rapidly burning. That might sound cruel to the civilians to you; but after all, it was the civilians who had hidden away the German soldier, so they are as much responsible for the crime as the man who pulled the trigger.

That afternoon our regiment went into reserve, so our battalion was designated to stay with regimental headquarters and guard them. At that time, we were still on the extreme southern flank of the Third Army's (or rather the fourth armored's) dash across Germany.

CHAPTER IX

The first night in reserve found our company dug-in on top of a high hill, far behind the front lines. As soon as we located our positions Doc Wandyg started off to get some hay for the bottom of his hole. He located a small barn not more than 50 yards behind us and started pulling some hay off the top of the pile when he noticed some movement underneath. Lifting up one bundle, he discovered a German soldier staring up at him with a startled expression on his race. Doc was unarmed, but the Kraut quickly hoped up and shouted, "I surrender." Wandyg then replied with an unrepeatable phrase and threw the startled Heinie out on the grass. Then he discovered another and another until altogether he grabbed five Germans out of the hay pile. Our combat troops had passed by there several days before and numerous rear echelon units had by-passed the Krauts without discovering them.

In spite of the five men, we felt comparatively safe that night, so our first platoon CP group decided to sleep in an air raid shelter 25 yards in front of our lines. The shelter was dry and had a stove in it, so it appealed to us much more than a damp foxhole out in the rain. The five of us - Lt. Schmutz, T/Sgt. Hambrick, S/Sgt. Chativoski, Pfc. Glen Williams, and I - all took turns pulling guard that night; for even though we did lose some of our sleep that way, we knew that whatever sleep we did get would be more beneficial than that which we would get sleeping all night in the rain.

The next morning Baker company was chosen to be division CP guard. We were formed into a task force with five tanks and three two-and-a-half ton trucks to provide transportation for our men. At that time, it was the luckiest break we could have asked for because we would be far away from the constant nagging of battalion and far away from the front lines. Another good point was that division let its guards sleep in houses while battalion made all its men sleep out in the open even in a safe reserve position. It was getting to be an old and sickening story of our taking a nice town at the end of the day and then having to move out on the high ground just outside of town while battalion slept in the comfort of the houses we had taken. With division, we could at least enjoy the luxury of living in a large town, for division CP seldom stayed in anything but the best cities.

Our first position as division guards found us in Fulda, where we stayed in some old, three-story German OCS (Officer Candidate School) barracks. It was really an excellent set-up, but we moved out that afternoon to another town about 20 miles ahead. There we enjoyed the luxury of living in some smaller houses with one house for each platoon. In that town I accidentally met up again with Bill Jaffe, the friend I had come overseas with, who was still with the Counter Intelligence Corps. I spent most of that evening with him and his friends and was very interested in the French soldiers they had working with them. One little fellow was an excellent cook and devoted his entire evening to cooking delicious French fries, which we devoured by the handful. He had formerly been a member of the FFI (Free French Underground during German occupation) and boastfully told of all the Germans he had killed with his bare hands.

Altogether we spent two wonderful, restful days with division. There was very little excitement, and we were really beginning to enjoy the life of the rear echelon. Our company kitchens were several hundred miles behind us, so we had to continue to eat "K" rations up until the end of the war, but outside of that life was very comfortable. I remember several homes we stayed in even boasted bath tubs, which we utilized for 24 hours a day. Of course, the only way to obtain hot water was to build a fire in the small boiler at the head of the tub, but at least it approached the standards of living we were once accustomed to.

The last city in which we acted as division guard was Suhle, a very large metropolis. En route to Suhle, the tank on which six of us were riding bogged down and threw a track in the middle of a large woods. After waiting several hours for transportation, we finally rejoined the company just as it was getting dark. Captain Stout wasn't in a very good mood when we arrived because the first platoon had been sent out to outpost the town, and Doc Wandyg and another squad leader were AWOL. Thinking that the company was settled for the night, the two men had started off in search for food. Then the division CIC learned from some prisoners that 1,200 fanatic Hitler Youth with weapons were supposed to attack Suhle at 2200 that night. So, our first platoon was sent out for an outpost on the edge of town. The fact that we had two of our own regiments in front of us didn't seem to affect their decision. The six of us were just loading onto one of the tanks which was to take us out to the rest of the platoon, when Doc came up carrying a large, heavy box.

As soon as we reached our destination he invited me down to his room. Thinking he had found some food, I quickly accepted. When I entered the room, I thought I was looking at a gun factory, for a large double bed was completely covered with brand new P-38 and Walther 7.65mm. (.32 cal.) pistols! He was chuckling at my amazement when he explained that in his search for food he had discovered the Walther Waffenfabrick (Walther Weapons Factory), and that was what had delayed him. Knowing that for some time I had been wanting a small pistol that I could conceal under my jacket in a shoulder holster (being a medic I was forbidden to carry one in plain sight), he handed me a gleaming new .32! I was so delighted I couldn't thank him enough, and to this day I still cherish that pistol. From that night on I wore that pistol under my left arm everywhere I went, and fortunately I have never had to use it.

Lt. Schmutz was fuming at Doc for being AWOL and was ready to bust him. Wandyg explained where he had been and presented him with a new P-38, something the lieutenant had been wanting for a long time. Doc was never busted, and the entire matter was dropped that evening. The next morning Doc repeated his performance to Captain Stout and presented him with a new Walther .32. That made everyone happy. Doc then presented every member of his squad with one of the pistols and still had half dozen of each kind left over to sell to the "rear echelon suckers."

Several days later, after we returned to the battalion, Doc was given a 90-day furlough to the States. He took well over a dozen pistols with him and intended to finance most of his time home with the profits from their sale.

Before our battalion returned to combat, Russel Basset, the third platoon runner, found some photo developing chemicals and we set up a darkroom in a small room of an ancient house. Since all the instructions for the chemicals were written in German, we anxiously waited to see how the first roll would turn out. Fortunately, the negatives came out in perfect condition, thereby solving my problem of what to do with the roll of film I had already taken.

Around April 18, our rest period came to an end and we returned to the line to relieve the third battalion in one of the most unusual types of combat I have ever been in.

CHAPTER X

On the morning we were to return to the line, I prepared myself for the usual type of combat such as we had experienced back in March. But I found things had changed greatly. In fact, ever since we broke through on March 13, the German army had been retreating all the time and was unable to organize into any kind of a smoothly functioning, fighting group. Instead, isolated units were left behind by the fleeing Krauts in an effort to delay us and give them time to reorganize. It was clear that some form of mechanized outfit was necessary to successfully pursue the enemy; but being an infantry division, we didn't possess enough of the desirable vehicles.

To make up for it, Colonel Gladding had a brainstorm that would permit us to move rapidly and still expose only a very small part of his men. His idea was to have a combat patrol composed of one platoon of men on two one-and-a-half-ton trucks plus two jeeps to lead the battalion by several miles and clear the route, so the rest of the men could follow. To my horror, he picked the first platoon of Baker Company to form the patrol. At first, I couldn't believe he was seriously considering placing such a small group so far out in front of any support that they would be completely without contact, but I found out as soon as I climbed onto one of the trucks that he intended to go through with his suicidal plan.

I'll never forget how my knees buckled under me and turned to rubber as we started out with the two trucks in the lead followed by the two jeeps! I had thought he would at least place the small and easily maneuverable jeeps out in front; for they were equipped with machine guns, and we had no automatic weapons. The 25 of us with packs and equipment were so crowded into those two vehicles that even a blind sniper could have hit six of us with just one shot; and there we were out in front of everyone, entirely on our own!

The first few hours of that morning were the most jittery I have ever had. Every curve, every tree, every embankment, every town, and every mound of earth meant a possible hiding place for the enemy; and my heart would turn over at each one of those obstacles we approached. By noon, though, my prayers were answered, and I was able to take control of myself a little better.

Only one unfortunate but unpreventable event happened that day, and that was the wounding of a little nine-year-old boy by one of our squad leaders. We had been bothered all day by resistance put up by Hitler youth kids in black uniforms and found they were just as dangerous and more fanatical than the regular German army soldiers. Several instances had been reported where small boys just barely able to lift a Panzerfaust had fired at tanks and blown themselves up along with the vehicle. Sgt. Keeley saw this one boy in black clothing running across a field about 500 yards away and took a pop shot at him.

The boy fell forward, and Keeley could see through his glasses the kid was too young for a Hitler youth, so he ran out and carried him to me. The boy was shot through the side under his right arm, but fortunately the bullet hadn't pierced his lung.

I was hoping we would be replaced by another platoon the next day, but we had done so exceptionally well that we were told to go out on patrol the second day. Our small group of men had taken over 40 miles of territory in that first day, so the colonel was well pleased. We all complained that since we were doing all the work for the battalion we should at least be able to sleep in houses or barns that night, but we received no reward at first and had to dig in with the rest of the company. Then the next day our platoon would have to get up and start out an hour earlier than the rest of the battalion to clear a path for them to follow.

Throughout the entire patrol our warmest thanks came from the thousands of Russians, Polish, French, Czech, Dutch and British prisoners we liberated; but their heart-felt greetings were enough for us. Often, those prisoners would station themselves at the entrance to a town to inform us whether it was defended or not and where we could find the Germans. They would all try to bum cigarettes from us and return the favor with whatever they had. One group of Frenchmen proudly presented us with several cases of soda that they had made, but it tasted more like a mixture of plain soda with water. Another small town we entered had strung up a rope of wild flowers across the road and showered us with more flowers as we rode by.

We discovered that, if given a chance, most of the Wehrmacht (volunteers army) and Volkstrum (draftees army) would surrender to us without a fight; but the SS troops invariably put up a struggle. Because it is the theoretical ambition of every SS man to die for the Vaterland (fatherland), we helped all those we encountered to fulfill that hope. We found that about 99 percent of the citizens of Germany felt the same way about the SS, and they were always glad to help us in their destruction.

Most of the towns we came to were guarded by road blocks at the entrance. These usually consisted of a diligently constructed log wall about 12 feet high. In between these towns we found the SS had constructed intermediate roadblocks by blowing down trees along the road, so they fell and blocked the way for our vehicles. In many cases, though, we discovered the civilians had removed the obstacles from their towns as soon as the SS men had left, thus speeding our progress.

We learned that the civilians in most of the rural towns were as sick of the war as we were and would do anything possible to speed its end. If we stayed in any town, we would make a dash for the hen houses and collect all the eggs. If we couldn't find enough there to give two or three to each man, we would ask for more from the cellars of the civilians. Then we would build a fire with the wood from the farmer's piles, fill our canteen cups with water, and hard boil the eggs. We soon found that the bouillon powder from our K rations made an excellent seasoning for the eggs. Frequently the women of the village would offer to fry the eggs with ham or bacon, and then we would really have a feast.

Because we had gone so far on our first day out, the next day's objective was only a short one, so the rest of the regiment could catch up with us. We reached our town by noon and were preparing to settle down for some well-earned rest when the colonel told us to load back on the trucks and go out on a reconnaissance patrol. The next large city, Regensburg (about eight miles away), was supposed to be taken by the 11th Armored Division, and the colonel wanted us to go up there and see if they had gone through yet.

Knowing that when the colonel gets a wild idea there is no talking him out of it, we solemnly re-trucked and drove off.

The first Kraut, who we found walking down a rail road track, was sixty years old so we only questioned him and turned him loose. However, we found out that Regensburg contained a large German army camp with several thousand Krauts. That put us all on the alert and as a result made most of the men trigger happy. Consequently, when we saw the next two Germans running through the woods, everyone opened fire and killed one. The other Heinie was hit in the seat of the pants so I treated him and put him on the back of our truck. He informed us that there was a large, well-armed road block about 500 yards up the road so the riflemen all got out and started walking towards it, leaving me with the prisoner.

Ten anxious minutes later I heard all hell break loose up the road as it seemed like every rifle in Germany opened fire simultaneously. To my ears it sounded like all American M-1's and machine guns firing, but there was so much noise a couple of German single shots could have slipped in without my hearing them. Then just as quickly as the racket had begun, it ended abruptly; and I could hear Lt. Schmutz's voice calling out the familiar, "Kommen Sie hier!" (come here!) Five minutes later the platoon came back leading 35 prisoners - two of them wounded. One of our fellows later explained that when they got within sight of the road block, they formed a long skirmish line with everyone firing his rifle from his hip as rapidly as he could. The men slowly walked towards the objective. Finally, someone saw a small white flag waving meekly from behind a large tree, so Lt. Schmutz ordered cease firing. Most of them came right out with their hands up, but three or four of them started back to get their packs (so they said). That's when the boys opened up again and wounded the other two Heinies.

From the road block we could see that the 11th Armored Division was just starting to enter the city so our mission was completed. Just as we were loading the Germans onto one truck and ourselves onto the other, it started pouring down rain, and we were soaked but proud as we victoriously rode into the battalion CP. Needless to say, the colonel was speechless when he saw the load of prisoners we had taken on our "reconnaissance" patrol, and to show his gratitude he told us we needn't dig in with Baker Company any more but could sleep in buildings every night from then on. Even though the patrol had been dangerous, it was worth it just to hear him say that. If fact, he was so pleased with the way we had been operating he made us the permanent spearhead for battalion! That was more than we had bargained for, but we had learned long ago that it was useless to argue with him.

I'll never forget the next day on the combat patrol as long as I live. When we started out in the morning, the first town we had to take was only one mile from the large city of Regensburg. Before we arrived on the scene, the 11th Armored Division had taken the city with a hard battle which destroyed a number of homes and factories. Many of the Germans must have fled from Regensburg to the town we were to take; and we, completely unaware of their presence, almost drove right into a beautiful trap.

About five hundred yards outside of the town we noticed a small mound of earth out in the middle of a field. Not paying any attention to it, we drove right on until we encountered another similar mound. Then we unloaded and started to investigate. To our surprise we found the mound was a hastily erected, fortified position that had been cleverly camouflaged. We realized that it would be costly to try to fight against such a position, so we decided to try strategy first. One of the fellows shouted, "Kommen Sie hier!" with no results. Again, he tried in vain. Finally, a half-dozen of our men raised their rifles to their hips and started walking slowly towards the mound, calling out for the occupants to surrender.

It must have taken a great deal of guts for our fellows to do that, for they made perfect targets. At any rate, they must have looked determined because when they were up to the fortification several heads popped up and pleaded, "Nichts shissen!" (Don't shoot!) After we accepted their surrender, Germans from nearby foxholes came running out towards us in large numbers. If we had tried to fight it out with that first group of men, we would have really had a battle on our hands; but when the Krauts saw we weren't going to kill them, they immediately surrendered.

As we walked up the road towards town we found more Germans coming down the road towards us to surrender. After a while we had to set up a collection point along the highway, and we would just tell the Heinies to keep on walking when they approached us to surrender. We even quit searching them for weapons and satisfied ourselves by opening their coats and looking at their wrists for watches as souvenirs. In the town square we found a whole building full of enemy troops with rifles and other weapons, so we had them pile up the firearms in a stack in the center of the square and then had one of their non-coms march them back down the road to our collection point, where two men guarded the entire group. Then we had to take each rifle, unload it, and smash it against a building to render it unusable by any other Germans.

We only had trouble with one Kraut, and he was an officer. A buck private in our platoon, who had absolutely no respect for any Germans, tried to take him prisoner; but the officer refused to be taken by an enlisted man. The GI settled that problem by ripping off the German's shoulder insignia and half his blouse. He also tried to prevent the private from taking his Luger pistol off his hip and received in return a swift kick in the groin. That changed his mind some; and when I saw him he was limping down the street with a rifle in his back, shoving him along.

We had just gotten inside a Gasthaus (Inn), preparing to get a snack to eat, when the colonel arrived and broke up our little party. He was too happy at our capture of the 200 prisoners to sharply reprimand us, but we had to go on with the attack. When the final scores were added up that day, our platoon, unassisted and without any casualties among our men, had advanced over 40 miles and had taken more than 400 prisoners. The colonel had been amazed by our feats of the first two days, but as time went on he became even more astonished at our actions.

For instance, there was the day he sent our little group of men into a small village to stay there by ourselves for the night. From its size, we felt sure it wouldn't be defended so we drove right up into the square. We were all dead tired and took our time about getting out of the trucks. I don't know what prompted me, but I asked one of the civilians standing nearby how many German soldiers there were in the town. "Viel soldaten!" he excitedly replied. Thinking I had misunderstood him I repeated my question only to receive the same answer that there were many soldiers in the town. Growing impatient, I demanded to know how many. He replied there were probably 150 or more of them! I gulped and told Lt. Schmutz; but by that time, I was too late.

From every house surrounding the square, mobs of Heinies came pouring out toward us with open arms. They tried to shake hands with all of us and by artful dodging

I avoided being hugged to death by one or two. Then down the four main streets huge columns of them came rushing towards us shouting, "Kamerad! Kamerad!" We couldn't believe that close to 200 Germans would surrender to the 25 of us when we were surrounded, but that's exactly what they wanted to do. None of them were armed or had packs so we started loading them onto trucks. Then they all decided that they wanted their packs and blankets, so we let them go back to their houses and barns to get them. We told them to hurry or they would be left behind, and you should have seen them run!

Finally, we thought we had them all loaded onto the two sagging trucks and started sending them off. Way down the road a handful of returning Krauts thought they were getting left behind, so they threw down their packs and equipment and ran as fast as they could. That event repeated itself several times until we had entirely too many prisoners to take back that night. So, we had to unload the men and place them in a school house and adjoining shed for the night. Finally, battalion picked them up in two-and-a-half ton trucks the next morning. Needless to say, the colonel couldn't believe his eyes when we started marching the prisoners out to the trucks.

In that town was a kind old Catholic priest, who I believe was instrumental in getting the 200 Germans to surrender to us. He seemed to be a friend to everyone and spoke to all the prisoners as they walked by his parish. Welcoming us and thanking us for our treatment of the prisoners, he invited us to sleep in his home that night. We thanked him for the invitation but explained that no American soldiers are allowed to sleep in the same house with civilians. "Not even the priest house?" was his astonished reply. We assured him that there were no exceptions to the rule and slept in his barn instead. He felt he had to do something for us, so he brought quantities of German bread and ersatz (artificial) coffee out to us late that night.

Another eye-opener for the colonel came two days later. Battalion was settled in its objective for the day so the colonel, as usual, sent us out to the surrounding towns to see if they were cleared. We had just started out when we saw a Heinie sleeping by the edge of the road. He was certainly surprised to wake up and find an American rifle poking him in the side! Then we continued on towards the next town, picking up several more prisoners en route.

When we finally reached the place, we drove right up to the square and unloaded. Almost the same thing happened all over again as scores of Krauts started filing out of a large barracks. There were several high-ranking officers, so they surrendered themselves and their troops to Lt. Schmutz. Altogether there were sixty prisoners so once again we were faced with a transportation problem. The German officer quickly solved that by offering the services of their truck. It was the charcoal burning type vehicle; so, while they were firing-up, we looted the barracks. I picked up a half-dozen rolls of 35mm. film for Captain Lindsey and some surgical instruments. Lt. Schmutz picked up several cash boxes containing pay rolls and turned them over to the proper authorities when we returned. Finally, the truck was ready to roll so we placed it at the end of the column with a German driving it. We rolled on into the next town where we found about three times as many men with four trucks. You can imagine the colonel's surprise when we finally rolled into battalion with that convoy of German trucks packed to the edges with prisoners!

The following day we reached our objective in the early afternoon and were going on ahead to clear the way when we ran into several road blocks. By-passing them, we captured several Reichsarbeitsdienst (the same as our CCC) prisoners, who told us that there was a company of them in the next patch of woods where they were finishing up a road block. We proceeded cautiously and captured about half the group; but we could see the rest of them by the road block, about 400 yards away across open terrain.

We were just starting to send one of our prisoners up to them to instruct them to surrender when the colonel drove up with all his tanks. He informed us that the objective had been changed and wanted to know what the delay was. When he found out, he insisted on pulling his tanks up into position and opening fire on the men guarding the road block. Before we could get by, the colonel had to call up two companies and charge the woods. If we had been allowed to use our psychological approach, both time and lives could have been saved.

It was so late when we finally passed the road block, battalion turned around and went back to their former positions. That was swell for us, for it meant we would have the next town all to ourselves. We finally stayed in a dentist's home, which was next door to the home of one of the most beautiful German women I have ever seen. The best part about her was that she spoke perfect English, having lived in Detroit for 17 years. Even though she had been back in Germany for over seven years, her accent was pure American with nothing else mixed in.

The next evening Baker Company was placed in a small town all by itself in front of battalion. That night Basset and I worked until after ten o'clock developing films, for we thought we would get a nice long night's rest. Around midnight, the entire company was alerted and ordered to march back to the town where battalion was located. Upon arriving there our platoon was loaded onto our trucks with the rest of the company on two-and-a-half ton trucks. We were then told our mission; and I had heard some suicidal missions before, but nothing like that one! Sixty miles ahead of us was a bridge which was vitally important and had to be secured intact. Our company was to race up there under cover of darkness and take and hold it until battalion could arrive. No one knew how long it would take the battalion to catch up, but Captain Stout thought we would be isolated for at least two days. So, rations for three days were carried. The first platoon, of course, would spearhead the drive, Captain Stout would follow us in his jeep, two M-8 reconnaissance cars would follow him, and the rest of the company would follow behind them. The only hopeful thought about the entire mission was that the 11th Armored Division was operating up in that area someplace and going parallel to our drive. We might possibly be able to follow their route part of the way, but no one knew for sure just where they were.

It was a cold morning with a heavy fog over the earth. My teeth were chattering but not entirely from the coldness. We followed a main highway that the 11th Armored Division had taken for about 20 miles and then branched out on our own. We didn't have any idea when we would run into any opposition so all we could do was hope the Krauts were all asleep. For all I know now we may have passed an entire German army that morning. But God was with us and we didn't see a single enemy soldier. To our surprise, just before we got to the bridge we started running into vehicles of another company of the armored outfit. The bridge had already been taken intact the night before, and we accomplished our "suicide" mission without even firing a shot! The first platoon was placed on the far side of the bridge to guard against a counter-attack, and the rest of the company returned to the friendly side of the river.

After we settled down, though, we found our troubles had just begun. The towns on both sides of the river were filled with liberated Czechoslovakian, Polish, Russian, and French prisoners - most of them in starving condition. A very brilliant Czech fellow, who could speak English and was formerly editor of one of the Czech national newspapers, told us that seven days earlier they had started marching with 5,000 prisoners. They were guarded by SS troops and forced to march 40 miles a day without any food. In fact, during the entire seven-day march, the Germans had not given them so much as one crumb of bread; and those who passed out or fell by the roadside were shot or clubbed to death by the SS. When we finally caught up with them there were only 800 prisoners left in that particular group. I know his story is true, for we saw the bodies of many prisoners lying beside the roads.

There were other groups of prisoners who had the same story to tell and all were badly malnourished. As soon as we liberated them they turned on their guards and beat or kicked them to death. When it finally got light enough to see, we found the bodies of several score SS along the road. Most of them had their skulls cracked open and looked like a coconut that has been cracked open with a hammer. After the guards were killed the prisoners started eating everything they could get their hands on in the way of food. Every few minutes we would hear the death cry of a chicken or a lamb ba-a-ing its last. They even slaughtered pigs, cows, horses, and domestic animals. As a result of the overeating, they all had diarrhea; and whenever they spotted my Red Cross brassard, they would come to me for medicine. Of course, I had nothing to give them.

Finally, a civilian came up to me and told me her little three-year-old daughter had been wounded in the fight for the city. I went to her house and found the poor kid had just a small tendon holding her right hand and part of her arm onto her body. I redressed the wound with a splint, gave her a shot of morphine, and went to find some way of evacuating her. Before I could leave the house, though, they brought in a Czech fellow with a bad knife wound in his left elbow. I applied a tourniquet and started back across the bridge, where I had seen several ambulances of the 11th Armored Division.

At the armored division's aid station, I learned that they had no means of moving the wounded, for their ambulances were all in use evacuating American patients. While I was talking to them, however, a small, clean cut looking fellow came up and addressed us in broken English. He explained that he was a Czech doctor and wanted to obtain medical supplies. All the aid station gave him was a surgical kit they had looted out of a Heinie hospital, so I asked the doctor to come look at the Czech patient I had. At least I could furnish him a limited supply of bandages from my aid kits.

Before we could reach the house where the two patients were, we were stopped at least a dozen times by other prisoners with ailments. One patient, a German civilian, was wounded through the chest; but all I could do was dress it and give him a shot of morphine.

Back at the house again I found a French doctor from Paris, who also volunteered to be my assistant. There I was, just a medic, with two doctors for assistants! They had been prisoners for four or five years and were not at all up to date on modern treatments of wounds. I tried to explain all about the new sulfa drugs, morphine syrettes, etc. as I used it, and all the two doctors could do was rave about how wonderful American medicine is. German medicine is in many ways primitive compared to ours, for they have only recently started using sulfapyradine and have no idea what penicillin is. As a result, most of their leg and arm wounds result in infection and amputations. I have visited several German hospitals, and the odor of gangrenous flesh is more than most people can stand.

It was really nice having two doctors for assistants, but there was so much confusion in the languages I was almost lost. As you know, my German is very limited, and my French is even worse. Fortunately, the Czech doctor spoke a little English, but I had to use French on the Parisian doctor and German on the civilians. Most of the other prisoners could speak a little German so I had to use that language on them. Before we had been in the town ten minutes, the recently liberated prisoners started begging food and cigarettes from us. Then they wanted to know when they could go home and a million other things. Because I wore the Red Cross they all brought their problems to me.

Finally, around noon, battalion arrived, and we were alerted to move out, much to my relief. They had only met a little resistance on their daylight trip to the bridge and had come right through. The Czech doctor, a really likable fellow and a really helpful assistant, begged me to let him go along with us. I tried to explain that we were going back into combat, and besides, there was no room on the trucks for him. He wouldn't accept my excuse and pleaded in his broken English, "Please, for me there is here nothing. To eat there is nothing. And besides, there is here all these - how do you say it - bad Russians. Please, I will not take up much room, and I want to help you." Then I told him it was up to Lt. Schmutz, for truthfully, I would have liked to have taken him along. Lt. Schmutz finally discouraged him, but before we left he talked me out of a Red Cross brassard. By that time the prisoners were starting to fight and kill each other so it was a relief to leave that town.

We had so many close calls and had so many miracles performed on those ten days of combat patrol that none of the men could have remained atheist very long. Every day, we would run into so many unseen dangers and stop just in time to avoid being completely annihilated that no one could attribute it to luck alone. The incidents are too numerous to tell all of them, but I'll give a few good examples.

One day we ran into a common road block constructed of logs - the kind we normally pulled right up to and found unmanned. For some reason or other - call it intuition if you like - Lt. Schmutz stopped a hundred yards before the block. There was nothing to make him think it was manned, but something told him to stop and send out men to investigate. Out they went and found several SS men waiting for a fight. They got it all right, but they didn't live to tell about it.

Then we proceeded on into town, and again something told him to stop instead of going on into the square. We had just unloaded when a Panzerfaust whizzed over one of the men's head and exploded near the truck. A BAR man emptied a clip at the Kraut and wounded him just in time. Then another German started running across the field to the left and two more carrying a machine gun went to the right. The Heinie on the left just got a few steps when he was knocked out of the picture by our fire. Halfway across the field the two on the right tried to set up their machine gun and spray us with lead. That's the last thing those two ever tried to do, for the entire platoon opened up on both of them.

Going on by that town we saw four large German trucks parked beside the road. For some strange reason Lt. Schmutz kept going towards them instead of stopping and charging. My heart was in my mouth, for I was positive the woods were full of Krauts from the trucks; but when we overtook the stalled vehicles we found they had been abandoned at least 12 hours earlier.

Another miraculous event was at Titling, Germany. We had been going along beautifully all morning without any trouble and were beginning to get too cocky for our own good. Titling was just over the top of the next hill, and we were preparing to ride right into it when someone noticed two Germans just at the crest of the hill. We stopped the trucks about 100 yards from them and a squad of men went up to capture them. When the prisoners returned to us they spilled the beans that the town was loaded with Heinies and SS. Sure enough, when we peeked over the hill at the town we could see the roads lined with foxholes and Germans dozing lazily beside them. There were even some civilian women out talking to them, and no one was aware of our presence. If we had ridden into that town or just over the hill in our two small trucks, we would have been slaughtered. But this way, we had the drop on them.

That was one occasion we needed cannon fire, so we called for the tanks. Then we had the machine gunners on our two jeeps set up their guns just on the crest of the hill, where they were protected, and get ready for the tanks to come up. Just as the krauts heard the approaching tanks they started running in circles and the machine guns opened up on them. By the time they got into their foxholes, the tanks were strung out along the edge of the hill and ready to have a picnic.

I saw the first tank open up with his 76mm. cannon, and he scored a direct hit in one of the holes, lifting both occupants about 20 feet into the air and showering equipment everywhere. The tank commanders manned the .50 caliber machine guns on the rear of the tanks and the lead really flew. When most of the men in the foxholes had been eliminated or had taken to houses, the tankers started working the town over with the cannons. With tracers and white phosphorous shells, they set half a dozen buildings on fire and then blasted as many more down with direct fire.

The entire town was full of Krauts, so the other two companies had to work for a change and clear it out. They captured one SS man dressed in all GI clothing with GI equipment, including an M-1 rifle. As soon as the colonel saw him he worked him over with a cat-of-nine-tails whip and ripped his clothing off. Then he had Lt. Croce, the battalion intelligence officer, bring him back to our platoon.

Since our only trouble as a combat patrol had come from the SS men, we had all come to hate them more than anyone else in the world. The men in the first platoon would never take an SS prisoner alive, no matter what it cost them. Lt. Croce ordered all the men to line up and each man to take a swing at the Heinie standing there in GI long underwear and stocking feet. Each time one of our men would take a swing, Lt. Croce would put in one of his; and what I mean, he really has a punch! In all the clips he took at the Kraut he never once failed to lift him off his feet. The Wehrmacht prisoners sitting nearby laughed every time the SS would whimper while pleading to the GI's, and they egged our men on all they could. Finally, when the SS fellow couldn't stand up any more, he was put on the front end of a jeep and taken back to the rear.

We never did hear for sure what happened to him, but a rumor reached us that he was taken back to two British soldiers who were prisoners of the SS for three years. I understand that when one of the Limeys heard how we had found the guy, he grabbed a grease gun and shot him right off the jeep.

Perhaps the above description sounds brutal to you, and I'm not saying I agree with the treatment he received. As Christians, we shouldn't treat any human like that, but was he to be considered a human? Are all the SS atrocities we read about human? How about the 5,000 prisoners of the Germans that were liquidated down to 800 men? And how about the American uniform he was wearing, which makes him a spy from the start? Perhaps the argument arises that all prisoners should be entitled to a trial, but he was never accepted as a prisoner of ours. As Lt. Croce, a really level-headed and humane fellow, put it, "Shooting is too good for him. Let him taste a little of the suffering he has caused others before he dies!" The one part I did not agree with during the whole procedure, though, was the idea of striking a man who is unable to fight back.

One other day, we encountered a lot of trouble with five SS men in a civilian automobile. Battalion was getting settled in its town for the night when we were sent out into the next town to see if everything was quiet up there. To our surprise, we didn't see a single white flag in the entire town, so we became suspicious that there were SS in the vicinity. Usually word would pass on down the line a day or two in advance that we were coming, and the white flags would be out to greet us - that is if there weren't any SS around. If the SS saw anything other than Nazi flags in a town they would break all the windows in the house and threaten to shoot the people if they put them back again.

Sure enough, when we got in the square of the village, all the people came out with white flags and told us that an hour before, five SS men in a car had come through and told them to remove the flags. They were very thankful to see us and quickly presented us with cups of coffee, sandwiches, bread, and other German foods. Apparently, everything was all right in the town, so we returned and reported in to battalion.

While we were awaiting further orders a messenger from the other town came roaring in on a motorcycle and informed us that the five SS men had returned and forced the people to remove the white flags again. Needless to say, that peeved us, so he hopped in our trucks and took off in search of them. We never did find them, but we saw their bodies later that evening. In their roaming around they picked up an SS officer with a sidecar motorcycle; so, with the driver of the motorcycle, that made seven of them. Then they made the mistake of driving into the town Charlie Company was occupying. They didn't discover that there were Americans there until it was too late, for the motorcycle was opposite one of the houses used as an outpost before it stopped.

Someone was sleeping on the guard system of Company C, for there was no one watching the road. One of the squad leaders stepped out of the front door of the house right into the motorcycle. Drawing his pistol, he snapped the trigger only to find a misfire. At the same time, the Kraut pulled the trigger on his P-38 and found another defective cartridge. Then the second Kraut sprayed the GI with a burp gun, just slightly wounding him, so the American fell in the street and played dead. Just as the SS stepped over to deliver the coup de grace, a machine gun opened up, killing both of the Germans.

By that time the rest of the company was alert and firing at the fleeing Krauts. A bazooka knocked the car out, and as the SS tried to run across the fields, they made easy targets for the GI 's. I didn't see the SS men until that evening, but the bodies were still lying where they had fallen. It certainly was more than a miracle that both of those pistols misfired at the same time and that none of our men were killed in the fight.

On another day, when we were out in front of battalion, we reached a series of complicated road blocks consisting of erected log piles, fallen trees, and craters in the road. The only amusing part of the whole affair was that the block had cut off two truckloads of retreating Krauts too, causing them to fall into our hands. We put them to work remaking the roads, but we could easily see that it would be a half-day's work filling in the holes. So, the colonel ordered us to take a path through the woods.

The first vehicle had just started up the trail when our truck got a flat tire and had to stop. The colonel, disgusted with all the delays, ordered the men to go on with just one truck and two jeeps, leaving us behind. As luck would have it, only the first one-and-a-half-ton truck (containing half our platoon), the colonel's jeep, and three tanks were able to make it through the woods before the road became too slippery, bogging down one tank and completely blocking the way for the rest of the column.

We were still 15 miles from our objective, so the colonel took the vehicles that got through with him and went on. The rest of the battalion had to turn around and wait for the engineers to construct the road. By the time that job was completed it was almost dark so the assistant battalion commander, Major Amarita, ordered our one truck to take the lead and go into the next large town, which the colonel and his men had by-passed. We were completely out of communication with the colonel and had no idea whether he had been taken prisoner or had passed out of range of the 600 radio he had.

After a restless night's sleep, the major sent our truck out alone to rejoin the rest of our group, which he supposed to be sitting on our objective. We all sweated out that trip; but when we discovered most of it followed a highway that had been taken by the 11th Armored Division, we relaxed a little. During the ride we had the pleasure of seeing a Luftwaffe pilot bail out of his airplane, which had been shot down by our ack-ack and crashed just ahead of us. A little later on that day we captured a Luftwaffe man who had just bailed out, and I suppose he was the same fellow whom we had seen before. I now have his pilot's helmet at home in my collection of souvenirs.

To return to the story, we finally reached the town that was our objective and found Colonel Gladding, the three tanks, and the rest of our men waiting there for us. Three of our men (including Paridis, the acting platoon sergeant) had been wounded and one killed in a German ambush the night before. One fellow, Perry, seemed to be only slightly wounded, but we learned several months later that he died en route to the hospital.

The day before we were to be relieved by another battalion, we ran into some Teller mines, those huge anti-tank mines that contain 12 pounds of TNT. At that time, we were still running parallel to the 11th Armored Division, with the other division sticking to the main highways and our division clearing the side roads and small towns. The 11th Armored Division hit the mines first, and I saw the remains of two jeeps that had been rendered unrecognizable by the explosion. All that was left was a burned, twisted mass of scrap metal. We shuddered as we pictured what would happen to our two lead vehicles if we were to strike one of the Tellers. Fortunately, we came through all right; but I thought sure my hair would turn gray before we got off those roads.

That night we entered a small town and were quickly warned by the civilians that four SS men had been through there just an hour before. In the next town the civilians informed us that the four SS had been through there on foot just a half-hour before. In the next village we found we were just fifteen minutes behind them and hot on their trail! To our great satisfaction, we learned in the next village that the SS had left just five minutes before, and sure enough, at the foot of the next hill we overtook them. I won't describe the battle any more than to say the Krauts tried to run and the fight was heavily one-sided. Of course, since the Germans were SS, it all ended up with four corpses in the farmer's field.

During the brief struggle with the four SS, I was enjoying the show by watching it from the side of the road. Most of the rifle shots were American and I didn't realize the Heinies were firing at all until I felt a stinging in my right hand and heard a loud zing go by me. I looked down and saw I had just miraculously been nicked on the back of my right hand, but whether it was a ricochet or a flying stone I'll never know. At any rate, I still consider myself very lucky to have had my hand in such a position that it was only scratched. I happened to mention what had happened to me when I was in the aid station two days later, and before I realized what had happened I was awarded a purple heart. I don't feel right about wearing it when I think of what a lot of guys had to do to get one, but now that I have it there is nothing I can do about it.

Fortunately, the 11th Armored Division cut in front of us after we got the four SS, for by doing so they spared the complete destruction of our combat patrol. In the next town, the Germans had set up numerous 88's, anti-tank guns, and cannons. The armored division lost four tanks and a score of men taking that town; and it looked like there, at last, we were beginning to run into the German army in strength. None of us were the least bit sorry that our battalion was being taken off the line then!

The next morning, May Day, our combat patrol was sent out to keep from making the colonel a liar. The night before, he had radioed in to regiment that we had crossed the Austrian border, and in doing so we held the record for being the first outfit in the division to do it. Early that morning we had to go out and cross the border, marking it plainly with road signs bearing the first battalion insignia. To our surprise, we awoke to find over an inch of snow covering the ground and a miniature blizzard blowing up. I had been acting radio man for the platoon since I was the only man who had any knowledge of the 300 radio. You will remember that, just before my transfer into the medics, I was assistant radio man. So that was the reason for my job as both aid man and radio operator on the combat patrol. I was to radio in just as soon as our unit crossed the border, so the colonel could feel safe about his false statement. When we reached the next town, in which the 11th Armored Division had such a bitter fight, we discovered that they hadn't even finished clearing the town with all their tanks and artillery. So, we had to stop 700 yards short of our objective. The colonel got the credit for crossing the border, though, so everyone was happy even though we didn't enter Austria until the next day.

For the next six days we just followed up the battalion which had relieved us. They weren't encountering much resistance, however, for the German armies had surrendered in both Italy and northern Germany and everyone was expecting Germany's complete surrender. It finally came on the night of May 7, when we were stuck in a jerk-water town named Gilowitz, near Hohenfurth, Czechoslovakia. The official VE Day didn't come until two days later, but we were told to cease firing on the seventh.

CHAPTER XI

Now that it is all over it feels strange looking back upon those nine months of world conflict that carried me across seven countries: England, France, Belgium, Luxembourg, Germany, Austria, and Czechoslovakia. Sitting alone in my room in this Austrian town, I have difficulty trying to recall those 165 days of actual combat, when I stopped being a civilized member of society and became a member of that well-known group of professional exterminators: the combat infantry. It seems far distant now, but there will remain traces of it for many years to come.

Out on the street, three or four ragged ex-members of the famous German Wehrmacht are slowly trudging up the street, leaning heavily forward to keep the huge packs from pulling them over backwards. Now a lumbering Wehrmacht truck is passing, loaded beyond capacity with German prisoners, defeated in both body and spirit. Perhaps they are going home for discharge, and perhaps they are laughing at us Americans who must remain here in uniform for many years to come. Perhaps they are being taken back to another camp for segregation into groups of war criminals awaiting trial or harmless labor gangs.

The truck is out of sight now, but it has left behind in my mind a fresh recollection of those seven months. Once again, I can feel the mixed emotions of combat - the straining of nerves beyond the bursting point, the deathlike tiredness, the momentary fear produced by a "near miss", the terrible horror of a diving plane, but mostly the mental fatigue caused by all of these emotions plus the never-ending missions at hand. Scores of men have tried to picture the infantry soldier in words, but they have all failed, and it was useless for them to even attempt such an impossible task. I would never attempt it, and those who have tried have only invited disbelief from outsiders and ridicule from the infantry itself. But that's as it should be, for the infantryman in the lines doesn't appreciate publicity, thanks, homage, or sympathy. For the most part, those men didn't ask for that branch of the service; but after living through the conflicts, they are proud of it. And now that it is over, they don't ask for gratitude or understanding from others. They simply want a chance to return to the civil world to take up where they left off.

Now that it is finished, I don't exactly know why I have written this brief autobiography with its inadequate accounts of the time I spent in combat. At times it was hard for me to determine whether it was good or bad luck that kept me from being among the average doughboys and being sent back to the hospitals after a few days of combat. Many times, especially during the freezing cold of winter, we unanimously agreed that it would be a blessing to receive a very minor illness or injury that would carry us back to the rear echelons where we were sure to have nothing but peace and quiet, beds, clean sheets, baths, hot food, and sleep.

You see, combat with the enemy produced more than physical fatigue - it produced, more seriously, an unconquerable mental fatigue. Had we been placed on a business-like basis where we could fight for eight hours a day and then go home at night to sleep and repair our minds for sixteen hours, it would have been endurable for most of us. But in combat there is no stopping. From one minute after midnight of a new day until midnight of that same day, we fought and moved onward. If we did stop, it wasn't for a rest because we had to remain on guard to hold our gains in the event of a counter-attack.

As a result, after several days of fighting, we all acquired a strange facial expression that is only closely resembled in civil life by the eyes of a dope fiend. Between the heaviest spasms of fighting it was possible to walk down a long column of men and not be seen by any of them. As they rested, their eyes assumed a glassy stare not unlike that of a dead man's.

The eyes told the whole story. By looking into an infantryman's eyes, it is possible to determine whether or not he has been in combat; and if so, approximately how long it has been since he was allowed a rest. The eyes look without seeing, as though someone had severed the nerve that carries sight impulses from the retina back to the brain. Those eyes that have feasted on nothing but death and destruction do not see the passer-by. They look at you as though to say, "I am a perpetual machine. I go on forever without rest." Their eyes are dim, and perhaps the owner sleeps; but the eyes remain open.

That's the whole story of combat - in the eyes. Even if the rest of the expressionless face were covered, one could imagine the features. From the eyes alone, one could imagine the open-hanging mouth and the bearded face that hasn't felt a razor for weeks.

But now it's over, and we can forget about the war, as we must eventually do. The papers say it wasn't so costly and that we only lost a million men in casualties. To me that seems impossible, for it seems like I have seen that many dead myself. It seems like I have seen that many of my friends killed beside me and that many more lying in forgotten ditches.

I have seen one of the graveyards in Normandy with its 10,000 white wooden crosses. It's beautiful to walk around that huge plot and find that no matter where you stand the crosses line themselves up in perfect, well-kept rows. Beneath each one of those white markers lies the remains of a fellow American. I wonder if those 10,000 have been forgotten by all but their families and friends. I wonder if 30 years from now there will be 10,000 more such crosses in the same land or in distant lands.

That will be the true test of whether we achieved our purpose in this war. It is true that we benefited much from this conflict. We have once again realized strong national unity, and we have made rapid advances in science. But the gains are greatly overpowered by the losses, and years from now those 10,000 beautiful white crosses will still be there.

THE END

EPILOGUE

Moraga, California
October 1995

Total Unconditional Surrender

The war was over! The German High Command formally agreed to unconditional surrender on May 9, 1945. Victory was ours! We could all go home.

So why was I still in Europe, writing my book, three months after the war ended? Good question, but first let me describe how close we came to be going back into combat in another part of the world!

We had already entered the Sudetenland region of Czechoslovakia as the war ended; and on the final days before total surrender, we were overwhelmed with hundreds, then thousands of German troops who were trying to escape the Russians by surrendering to us. We were dug-in in a farmer's field adjacent to a narrow Czech highway, not expecting enemy action because our battalion was in reserve. Without advance warning, a German motorcycle carrying a white flag rode up to our company outpost, and an officer in the sidecar started shouting in German at our point guard.

I was called to interpret and discovered that the officer was demanding a high-ranking American officer to accept his General's surrender of an entire German Division. Lt. Schmutz, our platoon leader, was intrigued by the thought that L/Col. Gladding, our Battalion Commander, would enjoy the ceremony, so he radioed the invitation to him. Gladding loved the idea of any ceremony, although the Germans hesitated because they would have preferred an American General--or at least a full colonel. I had to tell them their only choices were between a second lieutenant and a lieutenant colonel. Otherwise it was the Russians. They readily accepted Gladding! We designated a large field across the road from our platoon; and within minutes, tanks and armored vehicles began lining up there, followed by foot soldiers, artillery, mobile kitchens, staff cars, trucks and other vehicles and weapons of war. Upon arrival, each of them unloaded their firearms and live ammunition on our side of the road. Then they erected their camps with geometric precision on their side. By nightfall, our platoon of less than forty men had several thousand neighbors living across the street in their pristine tent city! Obviously, we were in an extremely vulnerable position if they should decide to change their minds!

This scenario was repeated more than once over the next few days, leaving us sufficiently jaded to give little thought to the process. Our division headquarters arranged the evacuation of prisoners, leaving their vehicles and other hardware to rust in the fields. With little else to do when not on guard duty, some of our men enjoyed racing the German vehicles up and down the hillsides until their fuel was depleted.

Military Police eventually took over the traffic control of surrendering Germans, so our battalion could move to the small town of, Friedburg, Czechoslovakia. There, we gradually shed our combat clothing as new uniforms arrived. We even enjoyed a few days with little more to do than calisthenics, hot meals, and softball! I was moved from Company B to my own quarters in the Battalion Aid Station, where we only worked for an hour or two daily holding Sick Call (urgent care clinic, conducted mainly by those of us classified as medical or surgical technicians). Eventually I was promoted to first sergeant of the unit with rank of Technical Sergeant.

Cessation of security measures meant I could use my camera, which my father shipped to me within days after the shooting stopped. He not only got the camera to me rapidly, he included several rolls of then scarce Kodachrome film for making color slides. I still have many postwar slides from Friedburg which were taken in May 1945, and they have faded very little in 50 years.

On to Japan

Our rest was short lived. Less than a month after victory over Germany, we were galvanized by the arrival of orders to move immediately to Fulda, Germany, to begin processing for redeployment to the Far East! We were slated for invasion of the Japanese mainland!

I won't try to describe the initial shock upon receiving those orders because I know that, difficult as it was for me, it was infinitely more distressing news for my parents. All of us had assumed that the hazards of combat had concluded with the defeat of Germany, completely forgetting that the war with Japan on the other side of the world was still continuing. Our troops were having great victories in the Pacific islands: surely, they would achieve unconditional surrender right after we did!

But we had forgotten about Japan, the homeland islands. Because of the great distances from our closest air bases and the limited range of 1940's bombers, Japan had not been intensively softened up with aerial attacks, as had been done for several years in Europe. Military analysts were certain that the Japanese would defend their mainland with the same level of suicidal intensity as displayed by kamikaze pilots. Their conclusion: victory over Japan was more than a year away; and, even under the best circumstances, it would exact unprecedented casualties.

So, we climbed into trucks for the long trip to Fulda and eventual return to combat. After the initial shock of learning that we were going to Japan, our general mood was one of resignation and acceptance, just as it had been to other disconcerting events in the service. The vast majority of us had not enlisted in the army; we had been drafted and were resigned to that fate, accepting it as the price of citizenship. We hadn't volunteered for the infantry but were resigned to the fact that we belonged to it. So now, in the back of those trucks, we had already accepted our assignment to Japan and were trying to make jokes about what fate we planned for the Emperor, just as we had previously planned the violation of Hitler.

In Fulda, we engaged in training for the different battle conditions which existed in the far East, such things as: making amphibious landings under fire, perfecting jungle warfare techniques, and confronting an enemy which did not observe the Geneva conventions, especially the one protecting aid-men while administering care to the wounded in combat. All medics were issued and trained in the use of hand guns and rifles. We received immunizations for the prevalent diseases in the Pacific, together with booster shots for everything else. We marched, drilled, and ran obstacle courses for physical conditioning. Then one afternoon, less than a month after we arrived, we received the best news possible: our orders for redeployment to Japan were cancelled!

Why were we and many other GI's relieved from assignment to Japan? Why were we excused from the hazards of becoming some of the estimated hundreds of thousands of fatalities to be incurred in an invasion of Japan, not to mention the wounded who would add up to the total estimate of one million casualties?

The answer was obvious to all of us back then, and it is still valid fifty years later: the atomic bomb! By June of 1945, when we were processing in Fulda, Top Secret decisions had already been made to bomb Hiroshima and Nagasaki. They were carried out on August sixth and ninth. And the very next day after Nagasaki, Japan accepted our terms for total, unconditional surrender! Period! End of war! No invasion of Japan! And no more casualties--on either side.

Only a relatively insignificant number of Japanese civilians died from those bombs compared with the number of both Americans and Japanese which would have been lost from continuation of the war for another year. And many more Japanese civilians would have become casualties from our air raids and eventual invasion of the Japanese Islands than did from those two bombs.

So, shed no tears for the historical revisionists who, fifty years later, appear to agonize with guilt over our dropping the bombs. They weren't in Fulda, staring at the renewed possibility of becoming a casualty of war! If guilt is to be perceived, let it be by the Japanese who started the conflict, without warning or declaration of war, by bombing Pearl Harbor and killing many thousands of US servicemen and dependents. I have been to Pearl Harbor and, while standing on the bridge of the Arizona Memorial, looked down at the rusting hulk of the battleship which still entombs the remains of more than 1000 sailors. And the Arizona is just one of dozens of ships destroyed there, along with their crews!

No! Harbor no guilt for our use of atomic bombs in 1945!

Army of Occupation

Instead of Japan, we were assigned to duty in the Army of Occupation and ordered to Peuerbach, Austria, a village near Linz, on the Danube River. Our role was to preserve peace in the surrendered lands. But peace in 1945 was strained from the beginning by the adversarial relationships between Communist Russia and the remaining allies, all of whom were democracies.

Germany and Austria were partitioned into western halves, with democratic governments, and eastern halves, with communist rule as puppets of Moscow. Fences were erected and manned by communist armed guards with orders to shoot any East Germans attempting to escape to the West. The Berlin Wall was erected to separate the two halves of the city, and many an East Berliner paid with his life trying to scale that wall.

In Austria, the Russian occupied area was just across the Danube River from Linz and was off limits to all but authorized US personnel on official business. One enterprising dentist in our outfit discovered the Russian soldiers' child-like fascination with mechanical trinkets during an official trip across the river. So, he had his brother in New York send him a dozen Mickey Mouse watches, which were snapped up by the Russians at exorbitant prices. He repeated his sales trips several times before the bridge over the Danube was finally closed to him.

We immediately established a warm rapport with the citizens of Peuerbach, who were just as outward-going and curious about us as we were with them. Our aid station and living quarters were in a 300-year old Gasthaus (Inn), which had masonry walls three feet thick. Bargaining for the exchange of goods and services began immediately. In the process, we became acquainted with each other, learned to respect each other, and lived together in the same village as neighbors.

The remainder of my eighteen months in Europe were spent in the same region of Austria near Linz, residing not only in Peuerbach but also in the larger city of Wels and in the town of Eferding. Even fifty years later, I can recall almost daily vignettes of not only the towns we lived in but exploratory visits we made to such beautiful areas as the Brenner pass, where I stood with one foot in Italy and the other in Austria; Salzburg, the Sound of Music city near the Alps; and Innsbruck with its picturesque alpine ski areas.

In August, I won a three-day trip to Paris, where I joined the French in celebrating the first anniversary of the liberation of Paris. There were parades down the Champs Elysees, concerts in L'Opera, and parties on every street corner. But to me, the fascination of Paris resulted from the commercial and self-conducted tours I took to see all the highlights of the city which we had read about in high school French classes. In just three days, I memorized the entire Metro (subway) system!

James Cutter (left) and fellow medics with captured German ambulance

Friedburg, Czechoslovakia. This photo shows five of us standing around the same vehicle, with me on the left and Tony Griggs on the right. The tallest one in the center is Bob Hosfford, one of our jeep drivers. The guy seated on the fender next to Griggs was our medical detachment clerk, Cpl. Thomas, to whom I am indebted for having kept a list of all the cities, towns, and countries where the aid station was located every time it stopped and set up at a semi-permanent location. He also did all of the records, reports, and paperwork. I don't know the name of the weapons carrier driver in the middle of our group.
Photo by James Cutter; caption by James Cutter

Fraternity pride in wartime – Teke magazine cover

Photo I took of Norman Bowne and I just before returning home from Europe. It was a posed B&W shot that I made with the self-timer on my Zeiss Ikonta for the cover of our national Teke Fraternity Magazine. We were holding a copy between us, and I was supposedly extolling the fraternity's virtues, which they used on the next month's cover to describe pledge recruiting efforts—even in foxholes.
Photo by James Cutter; caption by James Cutter

GIs on leave at the Arc de Triomphe, Paris, 1945

Our group of GIs in Paris, where I am the eighth from the right end of our tour group. On the left end is our tour guide, who spoke very good English.
Photo by unknown; caption by James Cutter

In January 1946, I was privileged to participate in the resumption of tourism in Switzerland by spending a week luxuriating in several of their finest resorts. The highlight was our stay for several nights in a luxury hotel on Mt. Jungfrau, the second highest mountain in Europe.

Two special occasions in Austria stand out in my memory. The first was my twenty-first birthday, the official coming of age in that era, much different from now. As children growing up, longing for adult freedoms, one of the most constant refrains we heard was, "Wait until you are twenty-one!" with the implication that all things would be available after that hallmark birthday. So, families celebrated the event together as a genuine coming-of-age. There I was, though, quartered in an unheated classroom of a high school building in the city of Wels, Austria, thousands of miles from family and home. My mother had mailed me a package of goodies and other gifts, which I shared with a few close friends. I cooked my own birthday dinner: Kraft Dinner (macaroni and cheese). And that was it.

James on the wreckage of Hitler's mountain retreat – Berchtesgaden, 1945

Our regiment arranged a special train from Wels to the Eagle's Nest, where Hitler not only had his mountaintop house, but also barracks for selected blue-eyed, blonde German girls and another similar barracks for similarly composed young SS troops— plus birthing facilities and nurseries—all to preserve the Aryan race!
Photo by James Cutter; caption by James Cutter

Hitler's window – Berchtesgaden, 1945

After the Allied capture of Hitler's retreat at Berchtesgaden, GIs often visited the ruins. This photo shows the shattered frame of his iconic picture window, with U.S. soldiers silhouetted against the same Alpine view he once commanded. The Berghof was later demolished to prevent it from becoming a Nazi shrine—making this view one that no longer exists.
Photo by James Cutter; caption by Gary Cutter

The other occasion was on Christmas eve in 1945. I had become acquainted with Dr. Schmidt, a thirty-something bacteriologist working in a privately-operated clinical laboratory in Wels. We often needed diagnostic tests for our patients' care, and the lab needed income. So, we started a mutually profitable relationship, which rapidly developed into a personal friendship. No one in the lab spoke English, and I was the only medic with any knowledge of German. Despite that, we communicated quite well with my pigeon German plus a few Latin phrases and lots of medical terminology. So, I became the permanent contact person with the lab, hand-carrying slides and vials of blood to them, translating their reports, and returning the results to our medical officer.

After a month or two of daily contacts, Dr. Schmidt and I were well acquainted on a more than business level of friendship. Still, I was surprised when he took me aside and very solemnly told me it would be a personal honor to both him and his wife if I would join them for a traditional Austrian dinner on Christmas Eve! Of course, I accepted and was given directions to their residence in an old palace, which had been subdivided temporarily into apartments.

On Christmas Eve I took a jeep and drove through snow drifts to an unfamiliar area on the outskirts of Wels. The palace was easy to find because of its immense size. The Schmidt's apartment consisted of one huge room with an ornamental plaster ceiling more than twenty feet high. Although the building was unheated, the room radiated warmth. In one end was a Christmas tree adorned with real candles, which the three of us lighted with great ceremony. There were many handmade ornaments related to the Advent Season, all of which were laboriously described to me in our improvised language.

In the background, a radio softly played Christmas music and carols throughout the evening. Silent Night was one of only two carols I knew all the words to in German, so I surprised my hosts by singing it along with the radio; and they immediately joined in to make it a trio. It was equally enjoyable later when we sang other carols simultaneously in two languages.

The symbolic Christmas Eve Dinner was the highlight of the evening, and to this day I continue to be amazed at the resourcefulness of my hosts in preparing it. Austrians were still going to bed hungry each day, and their shops were empty. Luxuries had been surrendered to the Nazis years earlier. But the Schmidt's improvised and served a veritable feast with veal as the main course.

The table was festively decorated with pine cones, sprigs of greenery, and bright red ribbons. Being a chemist as well as bacteriologist, Dr. Schmidt had created appropriately flavored wines before each of four courses plus an aperitif and after dinner liquor! All were crafted from various flavorings plus 190-proof medicinal alcohol, which I had donated to the lab earlier. At that age, I had no idea what wines or cordials should taste like, but all were pleasant and served in moderation during our four-hour meal by candlelight.

As midnight approached and I was saying goodnight, the radio again played the opening chords to Silent Night. The three of us spontaneously broke into song one final time as our Christmas wish for each other. There was, indeed, peace on earth to men of goodwill that Christmas.

To me, at a very impressionable age and thousands of miles away from home, it was a fairyland experience. And the memory remains the same today.

Finally, on March 26, 1946, it was my turn to board a slow freighter, the Hagerstown Victory, at Bremerhaven, Germany, bound for home! On such small vessels as Victory Ships, the yaw and pitch produced a high incidence of seasickness. Once again, I was spared that malady, but fewer than a dozen of us showed up for meals on several days. To get away from the stench, several of us spent each day far up in the prow of the ship, where the pitching motion was strongest, but we could read or relax while inhaling fresh ocean air!

Aboard the *Hagerstown Victory* – homeward bound, 1945

(James, third from the left) My favorite place for sitting and reading on the way home, next to my friend Hubbard from the 83rd Division. The bow of the ship provided some wind break. Despite the fact that there was a lot more up-and-down motion, which caused seasickness in some people, we both enjoyed that location for the trip back home. Photo by James Cutter; caption by James Cutter

Trans-Atlantic return from WWII

The favorite location of most of the GIs being returned home, so happy to be heading in that direction that the cold Atlantic did not dissuade them from sitting out in the sun and breathing fresh air, knowing that discharge from the Army would be theirs within a few more days or weeks.
Photo by James Cutter; caption by James Cutter

Approaching New York Harbor – the Statue of Liberty, 1945

The most welcome sight of all to us after two years absence from the states was the Statue of Liberty as we approached New York Harbor, and with Manhattan in the background.
Photo by James Cutter; caption by James Cutter

As we entered New York Harbor ten days later, the significance of safely returning home became a reality as we caught our first glimpse of the Statue of Liberty. She really is a beautiful sight when you have been away for eighteen months.

Despite bunks stacked three layers high, the troop train which returned us to St. Louis was a vast improvement over the French 40-and-8 boxcars! No, we didn't have dining cars, but the food really did taste better over US soil. Every one of us returned for seconds and thirds of one thing: fresh whole milk! We constantly yearned for milk while overseas, but dairy herds in Europe in the 1940's were not tested for tuberculosis. So, we could never enjoy fresh milk, only powdered, which at that time had all the taste appeal of cardboard!

Jefferson Barracks, although physically unchanged, looked as inviting as a weekend on the Riviera to us soon-to-be-civilians. The change in attitude and demeanor of the staff was most remarkable, especially when they looked at my jacket and saw the Combat Infantry Badge, the Purple Heart, the Bronze Star Medal, the European Theatre Medal with four battle stars, the European Victory Medal, and the exotic Croix de Guerre awarded to our division by the French Government. Or perhaps it was the stripes on my arm. What a difference two years can make!

My parents arrived that afternoon for a reunion which was almost as emotional as my departure had been eighteen months previously. Best of all, the now compassionate army issued overnight passes each day.

Discharge processing involved almost as many steps and as much paperwork as induction. In addition to recruiting sessions for enlistment in army reserves, lectures on rehabilitation, and discussions of veterans' benefits, we had to undergo a thorough physical to evaluate any service incurred disabilities.

At last, the event I had been anticipating for two years and nine days arrived: Discharge Day, April 9, 1946! But I have to admit, I wasn't prepared for the emotional wallop of the final proceedings.

The discharge ceremony was held in a small auditorium, called a Battalion Theatre back then, and my parents, sister, and two-year old nephew were in the audience. Our group of about 50 men, all of us relative strangers to each other, stood at attention in front of a podium, where a major conducted the brief ceremonies. He began by reading a letter to us from the President of the United States, our constitutional Commander in Chief, thanking us for our patriotic service to the country during its time of need. The major added his own words of appreciation in a warm speech, which he was probably delivering for the five-hundredth time. Then came the completely unexpected rush of emotion which I'm sure none of us had anticipated.

The major requested a moment of silence to honor our missing comrades. And then, out of nowhere, an organ began playing the National Anthem. Suddenly the memories flooded back. There was George Samsel, my old, intellectual, fox-hole buddy, who made me promise to take care of him if he got hit, only to succumb to a sniper's bullet on Easter Sunday. There was Tex Woodward, the trucking millionaire who was going to fly me to Texas to provide health care; instead a bullet ended his dreams for a "white discharge." There were the faces of Steve Stephens, Lucky Newman, and Phil Phillips. I saw Albert Stock, Harold Carmen, Edward Cauffield, Ralph Perry, and dozens of others who will never return. Then I saw many of the hundreds of other wounded who would come home with major disabilities. Finally, I remembered the dozens of close friendships

I had made during basic training and overseas service, friendships with men from all over the country who were returning home whole; men whom I would undoubtedly never see again.

With the final notes of the Star-Spangled Banner, the lump in my throat had become so large I wondered if I could even breathe around it. Then they faded away: the notes, the memories, and the melancholy. I had not been prepared for any emotion except elation at the moment of discharge, and I wondered about the others. "Dismissed!" the major commanded, and as we broke ranks I noticed moist eyes on many of the other hardened veterans.

The lump went away as my family stepped forward to take me home.

The lump returned when I visited Arlington National Cemetery in Washington DC several years ago. It appeared when I visited Punchbowl National Cemetery in Honolulu. It comes back when we drive past Golden Gate National Cemetery in San Bruno.

And it's there again right now, as I write these lines.

Reflections on 165 Days of Combat

Several months ago, while sorting through storage boxes, I came across the dog tags which I wore on a chain around my neck for more than two years. They are two identical plates of stainless steel, somewhat smaller than a business card, embossed with my name, army serial number, blood type, and religious preference. Mine are well burnished from wear because I was not permitted to remove them, even in the shower, for the entire period the army owned me. They were there for identification whenever needed, whether I was conscious, unconscious, or deceased.

It occurs to me that those dog tags are analogous to the memories recorded in "165 Days of Combat." Just as the dog tags were no longer germane to my existence after leaving the army, my descriptions of those days of combat were irrelevant to the interests and responsibilities of my postwar life. I had no occasion to return to either the dog tags or the memoirs until this year, when semi-centennial celebrations of the war's end stimulated my renewed interest in what really went on in the mind of the nineteen-year old me. How convenient that much of it was recorded in my own words of the times and saved all these years by my parents, initially, and then by my sister, who handed me the original copy just this year.

After refreshing my memories of those wartime experiences, I have reconsidered several questions which were repeatedly asked of me right after discharge from the army. Surprisingly, I find that none of the answers have changed since my twenties, and I can answer them now with even greater conviction than before.

Did my army experiences have an adverse influence on me? No, not in their ultimate effects upon me, although I confess that I perceived some of them to be adverse at the time. I used to sum up my time in the army with a statement that, having survived combat and the total army experience, I am a better person for having done so. I remain even more convinced of that now, fifty years later.

Did the war really change me in any way? Of course it did: in every way. On discharge, I wasn't the same kid who got drafted. But doesn't everyone change when maturing from age nineteen to twenty-one? Yes, but for me, an unfathomable amount of change occurred on December 1, 1944, my first day of combat. Thereafter, changes continued at an unprecedented rate for the remaining 164 days. On discharge, I was indeed changed, both deeply and superficially; physically and spiritually.

There were trivial, superficial changes, which others could readily observe. For example: I haven't been hunting since the end of the war, or even target practicing. Why? For one thing, I still cringe inwardly at the sound of gun fire, soft or loud. But more important, there's no longer any sport for me in pointing a rifle at something which can't escape; at something else which will die for no good reason. This is not a judgment against anyone else who enjoys the sport. After all, I used to.

Then there were deeper, more basic changes which I could share only with intimate acquaintances, and then only when sure of the sincerity of the questioner. I recognize them as profound changes in my personal relationships on three levels: with others, with myself, and with God.

Relationships with others? Yes, every minute of my time in the army was spent becoming acquainted with what I described in the Prologue as "an absurdly heterogeneous mixture of cultures, economic levels, and social strata." Developing relationships? It goes much deeper than that. When you share a foxhole with someone, your life depends upon his being able and willing to stay awake during his turn on guard duty, and vice versa, even though you are both dead tired and haven't slept for two days. Otherwise, one hand grenade ends the war for both of you. Culture, economics, and social strata are irrelevant to the total dependency relationship established in combat.

Relationship with myself? The solitary hours of combat more intensely motivated introspection than any other period of my life. There are no excuses or diversions to postpone the urgency of life's decisions when you are flat on the ground waiting for the next round to come in. And the will to make something worthwhile of this life - if I survive - is never more compelling!

Relationship with God? I always had a good one, from early childhood, having seldom missed going to both Sunday School and church each week. God was the principal resource for my decision to redirect my preparations for a career in engineering to one in medicine. But it was an immature relationship until experiences in combat convinced me of His existence within myself, not somewhere up in the sky; revealed to me that He has been there since my birth; and assured me of His continuing presence in eternity. " . . . I shall fear no evil, for thou art with me," the psalmist wrote. I memorized that verse in childhood. Combat taught me its real meaning fifty years ago. And it remains undiminished today.

That's the reflection which convinced me that I am a better person for having survived combat. How fortunate are others who gain those convictions without 165 Days of Combat!

Letters to Home

Why does this letter - and all the letters I wrote following basic training - begin with a salutation to my mother, only, rather than the "Dear Folks," which I used before and after the war? As a result of experiences during World War I, my dad retained doubts about the credibility of army communications with the civilian population. He understood the need for censorship but felt that information of significance to family members could readily be coded into the body of a letter without revealing its presence. He devised an easily remembered code for doing so, together with a means for indicating its use by changing the wording of the salutation. Un-coded letters would always begin with, "Dear Mother." Any change in that salutation, such as "Dear Folks," or "Dear Mother and Father," would indicate an encoded message.

---

29 September 1944

Dear Mother,

Your letter today was wonderful. Thanks for all the swell things you said, and I hope I can always live up to your highest expectations.

You know, mother, there is one thing about my going across that makes things look brighter to me; and that's this: things could be much worse. Things could be a whole lot worse, and I thank God that they aren't. I could be going over to Japan, where the fighting is lots dirtier and lots worse. At least the Germans signed the Geneva treaty, and we are finding out that they are living up to it. So, you see things could be a lot worse - at least I think so.

Well, mother, this is the last really personal letter between us. I'll keep on writing more to you, but a censor will read them also. There's only one last thing I want to ask of you, mother, and I want you to promise me that you'll do it. At least try to do it, and in your letters make me think that you are doing it. That request is this: keep your chin up, and always look at the brightest side of whatever predicament I may be in! That may sound like a childish and impossible request, but I mean it with all seriousness. There are always two ways to look at everything, and I want you to always look at things from the most cheerful and reassuring side. I'm going to be looking at things that way, and I want to be able to feel that someone else is too. And if nothing else looks bright, I'm going to look to the future - going to school at Drury, going to medical school, and going to work on my own with a MD degree!

Love,

Jim

Handwriting in the margin of this letter read, "You will never know how much these letters did help Jim." Signed, "Mother."

---

25 September 1944

Dear Mother,

I tried to explain to you about my going overseas on the phone tonight, but with the combination of a public audience and MP's listening on the wires I'm afraid I just made matters worse. I felt I had to call, though, since I promised I would let you know when to stop sending packages.

From now on, mother, I'm going to make it a policy of mine to tell you everything that happens to me - straight from the shoulder. At first, I thought it might be best to cushion the shock of anything that happens to me or is to happen to me, but I realize now that it is best to receive news - both good and bad - all at once instead of stringing it out. So, from now on you'll know that what I'm telling you is everything I know (within censorship limits). I realize that my going across is even worse on you than on me; for I can understand the situation ahead of me, and to you this game of war is a hopelessly confused mess which the world has gotten itself into.

Yes, I'm going across, mother, but it doesn't frighten me. And it shouldn't frighten you either. Remember the letter I wrote to you three years ago telling you about my desire to become a doctor? I tried to explain my philosophy of life in it and my belief that God placed me here on earth for a purpose. Since I've been in the army no matter how tough the going has gotten I've never lost or questioned this belief. And I believe my purpose in life is to help other people (as a doctor) in order to make the earth a better place for others to live in because I've been here. I say that I can do this best by being a doctor, but I may be wrong. God may have some other plans for me to accomplish my mission. When the time comes I will know, and I am confident that He wants me as a doctor. I'm going to attain this ambition no matter how long it takes.

Then why, you may ask, am I in the army now instead of in school? I think I know why: I'm learning more about people here than I could ever learn any other place. And to me, being with other people is living! That's the only way I've been able to take and enjoy army life.

My going overseas is part of my life, and I know it's going to be a wonderful experience. I'm going to learn more over there than I possibly could anywhere else. And it's going to help me to become a better doctor when I come back. If it wasn't going to help me in life, why else would God send me over.

Mother, I have absolute faith in the future, and I am happy for it. You must have the same undying faith, or you will never have peace while I'm gone. Remember, I'm not worried so you shouldn't be. Remember too, that whatever happens now may look dismal, but in the end, things will be the better for it. That has always happened before and will continue to happen.

I'm going to be gone from you for a long time, perhaps, but my thoughts will always be with you. Mother, I owe everything I have had in life to you and father. While I was young I couldn't realize this, and I may have hurt you deeply with something I said or did. If this is true, please forgive me. Everything I am today I owe to you. I hope you are not disappointed. My life thus far has been a wonderful experience for me at your expense, but now it is my turn to start repaying you for everything you have done. I understand all the wonderful things you two have done for me and all the advantages you have given me; and I'm grateful. To this I can't simply say thanks. I will express my appreciation to you by my actions throughout the rest of my life. However, right now I want you to understand that I realize all the wonderful things you have done for me and all the suffering you have gone through on my account.

Well, good-night now mother, and remember everything I've written. No matter how bad things may look now things will be better in the future. It won't be so very long until I'll be back with you again; and remember that in the meantime I'm enjoying myself.

Love,

Jim

---

12 April 1945

Dear Mother,

Here is another beautiful day - the kind that makes you want to get out in the sun and just soak it in. And that's just what I intend to do.

One of the fellows from my platoon received the best surprise of his life today - a 45-day furlough home. His name is "Doc" Wandyg and he's from Detroit, Michigan. I asked him to phone you (collect) when he got home so don't be surprised if you hear from him. He says he wouldn't know what to tell you, but I assured him you would pump him full of questions. I'm sure I have mentioned him before in my letters, for he is a second "Sergeant York." He has more guts and less sense of personal danger than anyone I have ever seen - yet he is anything but the "hero" type. He is a little sawed-off looking guy who lets his beard grow when we are on the line until it is about an inch long. He has been recommended for the congressional medal of honor for single handedly eliminating nine Krauts who were snipers at the start of this present drive.

Besides being a guy who hates the guts of all Germans, he is a screw-ball and cuts up all the time. A month ago, our platoon was leading a dawn attack and Doc (a squad leader) was leading for our platoon (as usual). It was still dark, and he hit a trip wire on a booby trap. It was a delayed action mine, so he dove for the ground when he heard it sizzle. Instead of landing flat he caught his stomach on a log - which left his rear end sticking up in the air. After the explosion word came back to me that "Doc got it" so I ran up to fix him up. When I got there, he had already gone ahead with the attack and wouldn't let me touch him. An hour later, when it was all over, I found and removed a piece of shrapnel from an unmentionable part of his anatomy. He was embarrassed when I gave him a purple heart for it a week later. He still doesn't know how he is going to explain to his girlfriend when she asks him where he got hit. However, we all agreed that if we ever captured Hitler we would invite him to kiss his scar!

"Doc" Wandyg, age 20 – squad leader, fearless and unforgettable

My father described Doc Wandyg as a one-man army. Doc was nominated for the Medal of Honor after single-handedly eliminating nine enemy snipers during a drive, and he often led dawn attacks from the front. Though he hated the enemy, he loved a good laugh—once injuring his backside and earning a Purple Heart in the most undignified of locations.
Photo by unknown; caption by Gary Cutter (based on James Cutter's letters)

Another thing I've seen "Doc" do time after time is go into a town we haven't gotten yet in search for German jam and bread. He always gets some and usually manages to get one or two Jerry snipers at the same time. What a guy!

Here I've been talking about "Doc" so long I forgot about my big surprise yesterday. I went down to the aid station and received three big packages. One was from you, one from Aunt Helen, and one from Mrs. Winkler (I sent her a request when she asked for it a month ago).1 They were all wonderfully packed full of delicious things to eat, and they all arrived in perfect condition. The toll house cookies you sent and the cheese crackers from Aunt Helen were not broken at all. The candy from Aunt D.2 and Grandma was delicious, and Aunt Helen's divinity and chocolate coated peppermints high-lighted the whole day. Everything was too wonderful for words, and I am still carrying a lot of it with me today. I am saving it for the five of us in first platoon headquarters. They are Lt. Schmutz, T/Sgt. Hambrick (platoon sergeant) S/Sgt. Sammy Chativoski (platoon guide), and Pfc. Glenn Williams. We all sleep together and stick together. Mrs. Winkler sent a Mavrakos fruit cake and box of Mavrakos caramels. Wasn't that nice of her? She is Lee Winkler's mother.

I have letters of yours from March 9, 17, 19, 21, 24, and 26 to answer. I also have a letter from Aunt Dorothy to answer the first time I have a chance. It is wonderful to receive mail at a time like this even though I seldom have a chance to answer. I have over 25 letters waiting for answers now. The only person I have written since our jump-off for the Rhine March 13, is you.

Those eggs the chickens are laying sound wonderful. We really fight for them over here. Two days ago, one of the fellows in our platoon put his chair in front of the chicken house and waited for two hours for a hen to lay. Then he was called to the CP to get paid, and while he was gone I heard the old hen cackle. So, Cutter had a fried egg for supper!

Yes, we were one of the first to cross the Rhine River. We did it at night over a bridge the engineers had erected. The simplicity of the operation was astonishing to everyone. Everyone over here is satisfied that there will never be an unconditional surrender with the Germans and that we will have to kill or capture every one of them. We are ready to do just that, and prisoners still tell us they don't think the war can last more than 3 or 4 weeks more. I just hope we aren't chosen to clean out the Bavarian Alps. I expect to see fighting still going on down there 3 or 4 months from now. And it will be all infantry fighting!

I think I hated to leave Dick more than he hated to see me go. I did have a wonderful time with him! It was certainly worth risking a court martial and being busted to see him.

Love,

Jim

Webster News-Times, Webster Groves, Missouri Thursday, April 19, 1945

Written to my parents as a rambling, twenty-three-page letter, the following narrative was published in our hometown weekly newspaper. I wrote it as an informal letter home during a lull in combat while in a German bunker in Saarlouis, Germany. Unfortunately, I did not review it for errors in grammar, syntax, and paragraphing. To my chagrin, the letter was published exactly as written!

IN SERVICE WITH OLD GLORY

Sgt. James A. Cutter, Infantryman,
Writes of Luxembourg Campaign

Sgt. James A. Cutter, infantryman, recently wrote his mother of his combat experiences while serving with the 26th Division in the Luxembourg campaign. He is the son of Mr. and Mrs. A. L. Cutter, 620 Fairview Avenue. The letter reads:

5 February 1945
Germany

Dear Mother,

Well, now it can be told. It has been two weeks since we were in combat in Luxembourg, so I am now free to write anything I want to about our campaign there, which was an interesting and entirely different type of fighting as compared to the sloppy, muddy combat in the Saar Valley last fall. You have asked me time and again to tell you just what it is like in front line combat so in this letter I will try to give you a little clearer picture.

You remember that last December 12 we were relieved from combat at Gros Redershon (that's spelled wrong, I know) and pulled back to Metz for at least a month of rest and reorganization. I can't tell you how badly we needed that rest, for our company was really shot to pieces. In fact, our whole company was just a little larger than a squad. Metz was a wonderful place where we enjoyed full garrison life. We slept in double-decker bunks in old German barracks (which were rather shot to pieces by the war), enjoyed meals better than any camps back in the states, and even carried on a training program of close order drill, calisthenics, and weapon firing. Everything was fine and dandy until Von Rundstedt started his winter push through Belgium. We had just received a bunch of green replacements and were completely disorganized when one night (I think it was Dec. 20) about 10:00 we received orders to be ready to move out at 0600 the next morning. There we were with about 150 men who hadn't been with us 24 hours (most of them had just transferred out of artillery, ordinance, and engineers and hadn't had one day's infantry training) trying to organize squads, platoons, and sections and get all equipment and rations (which had to be drawn through division) issued in time to roll at 0600. I had just received my promotion and was supposed to be a mortar squad leader, but luckily in the confusion of things my name was overlooked, and I was made a runner. Of course, being one of the very few non-coms and old men in the company, I was up all night. Boy, that was one nightmare of a mess, and no one knew what squad or what platoon he was in. But the next morning we were ready and on the trucks.

We arrived in Luxembourg that evening and hiked to a large forest where we dug-in and bivouacked. Luckily the weather was foggy all that day, or I feel sure we would have been made a target for the German air corps the way we rode on those trucks. The next day the division reconnaissance unit was sent out to contact the enemy (no one knew just how far the bulge had progressed), and the following morning at 3:00 A.M. we moved into the attack during our first snow storm in Luxembourg. That morning we hiked 18 miles with full field equipment over some of the worst terrain I've seen. My hands were just about frozen, and my clothes froze to me after being soaked by the wet snow. We finally reached our positions that night and dug-in without a shot having been fired. Then came the heart breaking (but always expected) news. We had finished a beautiful foxhole and made up a nice warm bed when orders came to move out. We rolled our equipment and pulled out making perfect silhouette targets with a bright moon against a foot of snow. It was rather rough cross-country hiking, and we were uneasy when we found out the Germans were wearing all white snow suits. We walked 2 hours, failed to locate the unit we were supposed to and returned to our holes. All we had seen was a German patrol car (which turned around and fled) and around two dozen prisoners another outfit captured. I finally crawled in bed and got 3 hours sleep before we received orders to move out on the attack at 0300.

Again, we hiked for about three hours (through woods, mountains, etc.). By that time my feet were swollen and completely numb at a time when they should be warm from walking. Remembering how the doctor at the hospital had told me to get on sick call the first time I noticed trench foot returning, I told the sergeant about it and left the company when we reached the next town. That was Dec. 23, and we still hadn't fired a shot.

I was treated at the aid station and returned to the wrong regiment, so it was Christmas night before I rejoined the company. They were in Eschdorf, having fought their way in that afternoon and evening. That night and the following night we slept in a 3/4 destroyed farmhouse on the edge of town - the last nights in a house for almost a month. While we were in that town I happened to duck into a shelter with one of our company medics as we were being strafed by 3 German planes. By the way, 7 of our P-38's showed up a few minutes later and shot down all 3 Germans. Anyway, I happened to mention 3 years pre-med to him and he took me to the battalion surgeon to see about a transfer.

Wiltz, Luxembourg

Following all night attack in woods near Wiltz Luxembourg, Infantrymen of the 104th Infantry Regiment 26th Division, return to their own positions on January 14, 1945. Signal Corps Photo #ETO-HQ-45-8018, 166 Sig Photo Co. #SC 270909
Photo and original caption by U.S. Army Signal Corps

Additional caption by Gary Cutter: James's family believes the second soldier, seemingly wearing round-rimmed glasses, strongly resembles James in both face and stance—supported by the photo's location and date.

I remember the day we moved into Eschdorf. Eight of us were resting up against a building alongside the road when 2 planes flew overhead fairly low. Never having been bothered by the Luftwaffe in France, I didn't pay any attention to them until I heard what sounded like a string of firecrackers going off and saw the cement being chipped off the wall just a few feet above my head. Man, I really hit the dirt in a hurry and started crawling under a wagon. Then the second plane roared down and sprayed us with lead. Fortunately, they didn't hit anyone, but by the time they circled for a second try we were all inside buildings and the place looked deserted. About five minutes later we had the pleasure of seeing those 2 planes knocked out by our own ack-ack units.

The next evening, we moved out again and hiked about 10 more miles against a heavy snow with a brilliant moon. Luckily, we only ran into one sniper that night, and he missed as he fired his last shots. We finally dug-in (try digging in frozen ground through a foot of snow with a small hand shovel some time - it's fun) around midnight on the edge of the burning town of Kaundorf in Luxembourg (about 6 miles SE of Wiltz).

Getting up at daybreak the next day, we shoved off through the thickest pine woods, heaviest snow, and steepest hills I had yet seen. For 5 solid hours we pushed along, trying to make a path through the heavy woods. We didn't take the roads because it would expose us too much, but finally that afternoon we decided we would have to. After only 10 minutes on the road we ran into trouble. I was up front, and we were just rounding a sharp turn when we heard a tank coming. It was so close we didn't have time to run for cover, so we froze on the road and radioed the rear of the column to take for the woods. As the tank rounded the bend he ran square into about 30 of us with rifles pointed right at him. We were helpless, for our small arms would just bounce off its sides and we were like fish in a barrel for his machine guns. Also, that long 88-mm. cannon on the front of the tank looked as big as a 16-inch coast gun as it pointed right at my head. We must have looked pretty determined, though, for it came to an abrupt stop and four German heads popped out shouting "Kamerad, Kamerad!" So, we stripped them of souvenirs, put the driver back inside the tank (which was carrying a full load of ammunition) with a GI guard, and drove the tank back to town with the other Germans marching in front of it with their hands clasped on top of their heads. I would give anything for a picture of that - those "supermen" were really a miserable sight to see. By that time the battalion C. O. decided we had gotten far enough, for we were out on our own at least two miles ahead of any support in an area that we later found was thick with Jerries. We dug in for the night; but you guessed it - we didn't sleep in those holes - at least not right away. Instead, we moved out to contact the company on our right. After hunting for over six hours in the dark we discovered they weren't in position where they should have been, so we pulled back to our old holes at about 4:00 A. M. and tried to get some sleep. The next afternoon we moved out for an evening's adventure I'll never forget.

Our orders were to move to a position and tie in with the right flank of another company. Reconnaissance had showed that the woods we were to move through were cleared of Germans, but we soon found out differently. It was one of those still nights with a full moon and we made perfect targets against the white snow. Besides, the Jerries were all wearing white snow capes which are perfect camouflage at night. En route to our new positions we passed several Nazi corpses and a good deal of German equipment, which didn't help to quiet our puzzled and anxious minds any. In other words, we were all jittery and trigger happy. We all had our weapons fully loaded with the safety off even though we had been assured there was no trouble ahead. It was just one of those uneasy nights that you probably can't understand.

At any rate, we met the company we were to tie into (which relieved us some) and were cutting across an open field for the next patch of woods which we were to occupy. Being a runner, I was the fourth or fifth man in line. Just as we got to within 25 yards of the woods a German machine gun opened up on us from the woods we were to occupy with direct, head-on fire. I felt the bullets brush by and instinctively fell flat on my face in the snow. Then I started feeling my body for blood, for I was positive they couldn't have missed. Strangely enough, they hadn't hit me! After satisfying myself on this point I began to realize that those tracers were still grazing me and that I had better get out of there right away. I turned around and started burrowing back towards the woods we had just left. It was just like the infiltration course in basic - only this time not in fun. I'll bet I scooped a couple of gallons of snow inside my shirt and coat, for I really kept flat I on the ground. When I reached the woods, I jumped up and ran in still farther, passing several German dug fox-holes. I was tempted to jump into one of them, but I remembered about booby traps just in time.

After the firing stopped an officer from the other company came around and warned us to stay on the edge of the woods as it was heavily mined. There I was in the middle of it and had to get out somehow. That's when I really began to sweat, for I couldn't back track out into the machine gun! Finally, I got up enough nerve to walk out, and luck was with me. I didn't hit a single mine! In fact, only one man in the entire company was wounded by the machine gun, but we were all split up and disorganized.

By that time, we were all mad, so we organized a patrol to clean out the machine gun nest. We thought there was just one lone gun in the woods, so we charged and were driven out with two casualties. Giving up the idea of capturing the woods at night, we dug in about 50 yards from it and spent a very uneasy night. All night long the company on our left received German counter attacks and piled up about 50 dead Jerries.

The next morning a platoon of tanks drove up to within 50 yards of the woods and blasted it with machine gun and cannon fire for over 30 minutes. We moved in right afterwards and found the woods contained a whole machine gun company of Germans - mostly dead - but we took about 8 dazed prisoners. The picture in the Grapevine shows the bazooka man who ran out to try to stop the tanks. He didn't get very far.

The woods was over 100 yards long, and I'm willing to bet there wasn't one tree in that whole woods that didn't have a shrapnel mark on it from the terrific shelling the tanks gave it. In the end shown in the picture (the end where my hole was) at least 50% of the trees were blown down or weakened so much they fell down in a few days. In fact, every time the wind blew another tree fell.

We found the whole woods full of equipment and foxholes, and there was every type of German machine gun imaginable there. The night before I had been sleeping just 20 yards from a German machine gun. It's a good thing we didn't know the size force they had in that woods or none of us would have slept!

The assistant radio man had been wounded the night before, so I took over his job - the first infantry work that I enjoyed at all. Sgt. Fairfield and I took over a German fox-hole and enlarged it for our use. Then we lined it with German blankets, covered ourselves with more German blankets, and threw a Jerry shelter half over our heads to keep the snow off. Then we settled down for a nice rest. All that afternoon and night they shelled us with mortars and 88's, and casualties were great. In fact, the one medic, T/3 Nagurney, was kept busy all afternoon and night.

The woods we were in was a valuable piece of ground for either side to hold since it was on the highest hill in that entire sector and was a perfect observation point. We had artillery observers with us all the time, and they could see to shell Wiltz from there.

We had hoped the Jerries would let up on shelling us after the first few days, but we received fire every day from Dec. 30 (when we moved in) until Jan 21 (when we moved out). They wounded an average of about two men every day with quite a few men killed. In other words, it was rather hot up there! One morning Nagurney and I were lying in our hole when 3 mortar shells, came within 5 feet of us. Then the fourth round landed on the edge of the hole and knocked a can of water from the ledge into our laps. It was a dud!

On Dec. 31, a runner came up and told me my transfer had come through and to report to the aid station. You know the rest from there. I spent a week training at the aid station and then returned to the company as an aid man.

I had a lot of patients up there on the hill, too; and many's the night I spent in my blacked-out foxhole patching up a man by candle light. I've had to handle everything from broken and amputated limbs to abdominal wounds and head wounds; but I'd rather not talk about that. It would sound gruesome to you where it is interesting to me. Besides, now that I've laid down my rifle for an aid kit I feel I am doing something more fitting to my philosophy of life - more beneficial.

Of course, it kept snowing most of the time in Luxembourg, until when we left we had several feet. The cold was good in one way, though. The wounded men never did bleed profusely; and I have even seen cases where men lived when in warmer weather they would have bled to death.

By the time we pulled out of the woods nearly every tree had been blown down that was near our foxhole - and there we were almost out in an open field. When we had first moved in we had been in the center of a thick forest. However, we used the fallen trees to cover our hole, which saved us more than once from flying shrapnel.

Well, now we have moved to a new sector in Germany; and believe me, we are really getting a good deal. We are (censored phrase) living in houses. In this area the Germans respect medics and do not fire at us. We are allowed to go within 10 yards of their positions to fix up wounded. We wear white cloth "sandwich boards" over our heads with large red crosses on our chests and back for easy identification. In fact, one day the Jerries ran out of medical supplies and came over to us under a red cross flag to borrow some. They got them, too. The Americans and Germans are really courteous and respectful in that way and still we have war! At times it seems like a big game where someone calls "time out," the game stops, the medics rush out and back, and then they go back to killing each other again. How futile it does seem!

Well, mother, there I have given you the complete story of a month of combat - sans the personal suffering which you have already over estimated in your letters. That foxhole on the hill was really warm, dry, and safe (thanks to all the German equipment). Nag, (short for Nagurney, the other aid man) and I spent many a long day in comfort up there.

I haven't padded this story a bit or omitted anything, so this is it - both the good and the bad. It should give you a clearer picture of what combat is like and should help to erase some of the horrible Hollywood ideas of the infantry from your mind. You see, it's really not so bad after all. True, I've had some pretty close ones, but every day I learn something, and everything I learn is going to help me get back home again.

When I first told Lt. Schmutz I had a 23-page letter for him to censor he wouldn't believe me. Now that he has finished reading it I expect to hear him call for an aspirin any minute now.

Love,

Jim

James back home in Missouri

James in his uniform standing for his dad's official welcome home portrait. In this picture you can see the patch of the 83rd Ohio National Guard Division up on my shoulder. The stripes are for Tech. Sergeant. The three stripes below were for one stripe for each six months of service and I had had 18 months of service when I was discharged. The ribbons on my chest represent medals that I had been awarded, the Purple Heart, the Bronze Star, the Victory in Europe Medal, the French Croix de Guerre unit citation and above those ribbons the Combat Infantry Badge.
Here are a couple of interesting statistics: When I entered the army in March 1944, I was 72" tall and weighed 133 pounds. Upon discharge two years later in April 1946, I was 72" tall and weighed 133 pounds! Net gain or loss: zero!
Photo by Arthur Cutter; caption by James Cutter

Bremerhaven, Germany
24 March 1946

Dear Mother,

Two years ago, next Sunday I entered the army, and at the same time I began my first long period away from home. Shortly thereafter I started writing letters home; and today I am writing my last letter to you, for we board ship tomorrow and sail Tuesday for the states.

A great deal has happened since that day two long years ago, mother, and the regular letters I have received from you have been a wonderful comfort and guide. Because of those letters I was never acutely bothered with homesickness during my army stay. Of course, I have always retained a great longing and anxiety to return to the home I left behind, but with your encouraging letters I was always able to adapt myself to whatever came along. It shames me to think back upon some of the trivial gripes and minor mishaps I complained of in some of my letters; but no matter how the tone of my letters changed, yours always remained the same. For that and many other things I will never be able to thank you enough.

Ten days from now will mark the end of my eighteenth month overseas. I'll never forget how hard it was to say good-bye to you that day in August 1944, at Union Station. Parting is never easy and departing for an unknown assignment in an unknown country didn't relieve the difficulty. I know how you felt that afternoon, and I'm proud you didn't show your emotions. I'm even prouder that during the six months I was in combat you were able to keep my moral up with your wonderfully optimistic letters.

In this, my last letter, I want to thank you for everything you have done for me in the army - for your letters, packages, guidance, prayers - everything. Here's hoping that in a couple of weeks I'll be home and better able to show you my appreciation.

Love,
Jim

About the Author

James Arthur Cutter, M.D. (1924–2014) was a physician, professor, anesthesiologist, and devoted family man. Born in St. Louis, Missouri, he served in World War II as part of Patton's 3rd Army, 26th "Yankee" Infantry Division. His wartime experiences—recorded in 1945 and preserved in this volume—reflect the perspective of a young soldier writing in the aftermath of intense combat.

Following the war, Cutter earned his medical degree from Washington University School of Medicine in 1951 and trained in anesthesiology at Brooke General Hospital in San Antonio. Over the next three decades, he distinguished himself in both academic and clinical practice. He served as a professor at the University of Buffalo and the University of Oklahoma, later becoming Chief of Anesthesia at Oklahoma and multiple institutions within the Kaiser Permanente system in Northern California. He also chaired Kaiser's Regional Chiefs of Anesthesia and contributed to leading medical journals in anesthesiology, surgery, and medical education.

Cutter was a Diplomate of the American Board of Anesthesiology and a Fellow of both the American College of Anesthesiologists and the American College of Chest Physicians.

A lifelong learner and passionate hobbyist, Cutter was a professional-grade photographer, an audiophile, and an early adopter of technology. He was married to Norma Gloria Zynda for 57 years, and together they raised seven children and welcomed sixteen grandchildren. His legacy lives on through his family, his contributions to medicine, and the words he left behind.

Photo by Keith Cutter

Dates & Unit Locations in Wartime

The following list is a rough approximation of my actual locations during wartime, showing the names of cities and villages nearest our combat positions in the field. Security precautions prevented us from carrying such records on our persons during combat, so I have reconstructed this list at the war's end using official records of our battalion's headquarters. They were always within a few miles of us. (Gary Cutter later noted possible errors and plotted the route on a contemporary map.)

October 1944:
 4 SS Nieu Amsterdam, North Atlantic
 13 Glasgow, Scotland
 14 Camp Delamere Park, England
 23 Southampton
 23 SS Antenor, English Channel

France

 26 Cherbourg (Omaha Beach)

November 1944:
 2 On train: Le Mans, Neufchateau, etc.
 23 Toul
 24 Nancy
 29 Grening

December 1944:

1	Wolfskirchen Woods, Wolfskirchen
2	Pisdorf (no longer exists, later became part of Sarrewerden in 1972)
4	Saare-Union
4	Oermingen
6	Kalhausen
7	Etting (Etting, 57412, France)
7	Achen
10	Gros-Rederching
11	Kalhausen
12	Metz

Luxembourg

20	Hobscheid
21	Eischen
22	Platen
23	Buschrodt
24	Grevels-Bresil
26	Eschdorf
28	Esch-sur-Sure
29	Kaundorf

January 1945:

21	Baschleiden
24	Noetrange
27	Pikard

Germany

28	Saarlautern (Saarlouis today)

February 1945:

France

13	Falch (error?)

Germany

16	Saarlautern (Saarlouis today)
19	Uberherrn

France

| 25 | Metz |
| 27 | Nancy |

Germany

| 28 | Gerlfanger |

March 1945:
6	Irsch
11	Serrig
15	Hamm (error?)
16	Saarholzbach
17	Reinbach (error?)
18	Thalexweiler
19	Niederlinxweiler
20	Ramstein
21	Waldleiningen
23	Gau-Heppenhausen
24	Oppenheim, crossed Rhine at 2330
25	Pfungstadt
26	Babenhausen
27	Obernau (error?)
28	Stockstadt
30	Kahl a. Main
31	Wittgenborn

April 1945:
1	Breitenbach (error?)
4	Istergiesel
5	Kaltennordheim
7	Meiningen
8	Schmeheim
11	Geisenheim (error?)
12	Goldisthal
13	Neuhaus (likely Neuhaus am Rennweg)
14	Steinbach
15	Plosen (Plosenmuhle?)
16	Wustenselbitz
18	Sparneck
19	Weissenstadt (Weißenstadt)
20	Erbendorf
21	Parkstein
22	Weiden (Constituency of Weiden likely)
23	Dieterskirchen
24	Roding
25	Elisabethszell

26	Kockersried
27	Bischofsmais
28	Zenting
29	Tittling
30	Krinning

May 1945:
1	Kasberg, 94110 Wegscheid
2	Sarleinsbach
4	Witzersdorf
5	Altenschlag

Czechoslovakia

| 6 | Hohenfurth (now Vyssi Brod, Czech Republic) |
| 8 | Gilowitz (error?) |

Austria

| 22 | Friedburg |

Index

[WIA] = Wounded in Action
[KIA] = Killed in Action

125